IF YOU LIKE HAMBURGER
BECAUSE IT'S EASY TO PREPARE,
ECONOMICAL AND NUTRITIOUS
—BUT YOUR FAMILY SAYS,

"NOT *AGAIN!*"

. . . the recipes in this book will keep every-body happy. They're all based on hamburger, but they're so varied that you can produce a brand-new menu surprise for every day of the year.

Want a one-dish meal to save washing up on a busy day? A new kind of sandwich for a cook-out? A sturdy meat pie for a hard-working husband? A casserole that can be stretched and stretched when unexpected guests drop in? They're all here, along with hundreds of other recipes suitable for any and every occasion.

Need any more good reasons for learning new ways to use hamburger? Of course not! You *know* your family will love it—in any of the 365 ways this book shows you how to cook it.

THE NEW HAM-BURGER COOKBOOK

DEBRA G. WOODFORD

CONTENTS

	Introduction	ix
1	Loaves for Loafers	11
2	Case That Casserole	27
3	Serve It in One Dish	41
4	Shades of Lord Sandwich!	58
5	You're in the Dough	71
6	Department of Interior Surprises	83
7	Soup's On	95
8	Quickies	108
9	Meat Balls Galore	113
10	Lamburgers	126
11	Viva Italia	138
	Index	153

THE NEW
HAMBURGER
COOKBOOK

INTRODUCTION

To MANY PEOPLE the word "hamburger" conjures up a picture of a limp, slightly browned piece of ground meat between two soft roll halves, oozing with onions, catsup, mustard and pickle slices. But to a cook who enjoys experimenting with this inexpensive but nutritious menu staple, hamburger is much more than that.

In the raw stage, hamburger has many different versions. The meat departments of supermarkets, good butchers, and reputable freezing concerns usually do not put more than 25% fat or suet in their hamburger. If you buy packaged meats at a supermarket, you can usually tell how much fat filler has been ground with the hamburger by the appearance. If the meat is a light pink, with lots of white flecks showing, beware! The fat content is probably high. If you buy it you will end up with 50% grease and only 50% meat protein.

To taste good, hamburger should contain no more than 12% to 25% fat. The presence of this moderate amount of fat adds to the meat's juiciness and flavor. Without any fat content, hamburger is dry and flavorless.

The color of good hamburger is like that of the loin in a T-bone steak—red and rich, slightly flecked with white. Good hamburger is ground from flank, brisket, portions of the shanks, neck meat, etc. Most hamburger is of a medium-coarse grind. If it is ground too fine, the structure of the meat is completely broken down and the result is a dry, flavorless dish.

The freshness of the meat is another prime factor to bear in mind in hamburger cookery. A reputable butcher never grinds the meat too long before he sells it. Good hamburger can keep its flavor and freshness for at least two or three days after you buy it. Always store it in a tightly covered glass, porcelain or plastic dish in the coldest spot in the refrigerator.

Hamburger can be frozen with great success. It is one of the few meats you can remove from the freezer stone hard and immediately start sautéing without making it lose its flavor. When freezing hamburger, remove it from the paper store bag and put it into an airtight plastic container. If you are going to freeze casserole dishes for future meals, always encase them in airtight plastic bags. Keeping air away from frozen foods is of the utmost importance.

If you make hamburger patties for freezing, be sure to layer each one in aluminum foil. When you have to rush, this eliminates waiting for thawing. You can separate the patties easily and start cooking them immediately. I also find those little plastic bags that come on a roll are wonderful for storing hamburger patties. With each patty encased in its own plastic bag, storage is simple after they are frozen. The little bags also permit you to take out one or two separate patties for a latecomer to dinner, or six or eight from your frozen cache without having to thaw the whole lot.

All of the recipes in this book are designed to serve four people with good healthy appetites. If you get into a spot where you find you have only one package of hamburger, and ten people to feed—remember hamburger is elastic in flavor; it can be stretched and stretched!

Many spices and flavorings are used in this book. Substitution of a spice can prove the downfall of an otherwise good dish. If you do not have the spice called for in your cabinet, it's better to skip the recipe than have to toss good food away uneaten. If you are not familiar with a spice or herb, put a little on the tip of your tongue to see if you find its flavor agreeable. If you don't care for it, that recipe is probably not for you.

In this day of high-protein diets, hamburger can be your nutritious, economical stand-by. After all, good hamburger is protein laden.

In fact, any way you look at it, hamburger is America's all-purpose meat!

Chapter I

LOAVES FOR LOAFERS

Meat loaves are excellent one-dish meals. And they need not be only for pot-luck occasions; they can come to the table with the elegance of a seven-rib crown roast. Meat loaves are easy to make, easy to serve, and easy to digest. They slice well, both hot and cold; if you have lunch carriers in your clan, they will enjoy meat loaf more than Bologna sandwiches.

Meat loaves are wonderful for people who like to loaf and take a day off from cooking. All you have to do is double the recipe, bake two loaves, freeze one and serve the other. Then when that day of freedom comes along, take out the frozen loaf early enough to let it thaw. You can serve it cold, if you can't get up enough strength to turn on the oven!

MEAT LOAF WITH CHEESE

2 pounds hamburger
¼ chopped onion, or ¼ cup dehydrated onion flakes, soaked in ¼ cup milk
2 eggs, slightly beaten
1 teaspoon salt
¼ teaspoon pepper
1 teaspoon celery seed
1½ cups whole milk
1 cup dry bread crumbs
¾ cup diced American cheese (reserve 10 pieces for the top)
¾ cup diced Swiss cheese (reserve 10 pieces for the top)
¼ teaspoon paprika

Mix all of the ingredients except the cheese and the paprika; stir well so that all are thoroughly mixed. Add the cheese (except for the reserved pieces) with a light hand so that you do not break up the pieces. Press the mixture into a well-greased baking tin. Slightly indent the center, and decorate with the pieces of cheese you have reserved; sprinkle with paprika. Put into a 350° F. preheated oven and bake for 1 hour. When removing from the loaf tin, be sure to loosen all four sides with a spatula before lifting out so the loaf will not crumble.

This loaf is excellent with mashed potatoes and frozen fresh peas arranged around the edge of the platter.

MILK-RICH MEAT LOAF

If some members of your family refuse to drink their quota of milk, this is a marvelous way to slip in an extra pint.

¼ teaspoon paprika
1 egg
1½ pounds ground veal, pork and beef (most supermarkets sell it packaged in equal portions of these three kinds of meat)
¼ cup flour
2 cups scalded milk
1 small onion, grated, or ¼ cup dehydrated onion, soaked in ¾ cup milk
2 cups soft bread crumbs
½ teaspoon salt
¼ teaspoon pepper
½ teaspoon Accent
⅛ teaspoon nutmeg
⅛ teaspoon cinnamon

A fluted type of mold is wonderful for this meat loaf; if you do not own one, a regular loaf tin will do. Butter all sides of the mold and sprinkle lightly with paprika. (Paprika gives a rich brown color to meat.) Beat the egg slightly and add to the meat mixture. Alternately add the flour and the scalded milk to the meat mixture. Add the onion, and work in the bread crumbs. Add the salt, pepper, Accent, nutmeg and cinnamon. Stir all well to mix the flavors thoroughly. Turn into greased mold form or baking tin.

Place mold in a pan of hot water in a preheated 350° F. oven. Bake for 1 hour, or until the center of the loaf is firm to the touch. Turn out on a warmed platter. Garnish with parsley and rings of boiled carrots, if desired.

WHEATIES MEAT LOAF WITH VEGETABLE SOUP

1½ pounds hamburger
¼ cup chopped onion
½ teaspoon salt
¼ teaspoon ground pepper
½ teaspoon Accent
2 cups Wheaties cereal
1 egg, beaten with 1 tablespoon water
1 can beef-vegetable soup

Mix all of the ingredients with the exception of the soup. Stir until all are well blended. Finally, fold in the soup, taking care that you do not mash the vegetables beyond identification.

Put into a greased loaf pan and bake in a preheated 350° F. oven for 1 hour, or until center of loaf is firm to the touch. Baste from time to time with the liquid which gathers around the loaf.

This loaf is very colorful when sliced. It is excellent served cold.

Variations:

Substitute 1 can cream of mushroom soup for the beef-vegetable soup.
Substitute 1 can cream of chicken soup for the beef vegetable soup.
Substitute 1 can cream of celery for beef vegetable soup.
For a wonderful flavor, add 3 tablespoons wheat germ.
Substitute corn flakes for Wheaties.
Substitute Cheerios for Wheaties.
Substitute 4 shredded wheat biscuits for Wheaties.
Substitute Rice Chex for Wheaties.

HAM-HAMBURGER MEAT LOAF

This is one of my favorite meat loaf recipes because it tastes so good in sandwiches. It blends well with either whole wheat or rye bread.

1½ pounds hamburger
1 pound ground ham (we usually ask the butcher to save boiled ham ends to grind for this)
2 eggs, beaten until lemon yellow
½ cup condensed milk
1 cup soft bread crumbs
¼ teaspoon pepper
¼ teaspoon dry mustard
1 teaspoon Accent
⅛ teaspoon ground cloves
4 slices pineapple
1 tablespoon brown sugar

Mix very thoroughly all of the ingredients except the pineapple and brown sugar. Form into a loaf and place in a buttered loaf tin. If your family likes a crisp outside on a loaf, this one can be made in an oblong shape and baked on a flat coffee-cake tin.

Place the pineapple slices on the top and hold them in place with toothpicks. Sprinkle the brown sugar over each slice. Place loaf in a preheated 350° F. oven and bake for 1 hour, or until firm to the touch.

Left-over ham can be frozen successfully. The next time you bake a big ham, freeze the scraps to use in this recipe.

RUSSIAN MEAT LOAF

1 cup rice
2 cups water
3 hard-boiled eggs
1 medium-sized onion, chopped fine
1 tablespoon butter
3 slices white bread, broken into coarse crumbs and moistened in ¼ cup water
1 pound hamburger
½ teaspoon monosodium glutamate
½ teaspoon salt
¼ teaspoon pepper

Boil the rice in the water for 15 minutes in a covered pan. At the end of this time the grains should be fluffy and tender. Rinse in warm water and drain thoroughly. Chop the hard-boiled eggs into coarse pieces so that they keep their yellow and white identity. Fold the eggs into the boiled rice. In a small pan, sauté the onion in the butter until it is transparent but not brown.

Mix the sautéed onion and the moistened bread crumbs with the hamburger. Add the monosodium glutamate, salt and pepper. Flatten the meat mixture on a piece of aluminum foil, making a circle about the size of a pie plate.

Place the rice and egg mixture in the middle of the meat circle. Using the foil for support, bring up the sides of the meat until the rice and egg mixture is completely hidden. Leave a small opening in the top of the foil for the steam to escape.

Place in a flat pan and bake in a preheated 350° F. oven for 45 minutes. Garnish with chopped parsley if you want additional color.

FRENCH MEAT LOAF WITH LEEK

Leek is an unusual vegetable which few but the French know how to use. If you want a meat loaf that is both different and delightful in flavor, try this one.

2 eggs, beaten to a lemon-yellow color
½ cup water
4 slices white bread with the crusts removed
½ cup chopped onion
1 can tomato soup
1 pound hamburger
½ teaspoon salt
¼ teaspoon pepper
⅛ teaspoon nutmeg
2 good-sized leeks

Beat the eggs, then add the water. Break up the bread and add to the egg-and-water mixture. Add the onion and ¼ of the can of tomato soup. Reserve the remainder of the soup until later. Add the meat to the softened bread mixture, along with the salt, pepper and nutmeg. Mix all very thoroughly and set aside.

Thoroughly butter the sides and bottom of a loaf tin. Wash the leeks and remove the harsh outer leaves. Cut into ⅛" slices. Line the bottom of the buttered loaf tin with slices of leek, reserving the rest of the slices until later.

Gently spoon the meat mixture into the loaf pan over the leek. Pour over the meat mixture the remainder of the tomato soup. Arrange the rest of the leek over the top. Place in a preheated 350° F. oven and bake for 1 hour.

This loaf is excellent served with plain boiled potatoes.

FESTIVE MEAT LOAF

Here is a meat loaf made with, of all things, fruit. There is a festive air about it, and an outstandingly different flavor.

1½ pounds hamburger
1 pound lean ground pork
1 teaspoon salt
¼ teaspoon pepper
2 eggs
1 teaspoon monosodium glutamate
4 cups soft bread crumbs

Filling

¾ cup seedless raisins
¼ cup dried apricots, cut into ⅛″ slices
½ cup chopped onion
¼ cup chopped parsley
¼ teaspoon sage
¼ teaspoon thyme
½ cup water or bouillon

Mix the meat, salt, pepper, eggs, monosodium glutamate and bread crumbs thoroughly. Spread on a sheet of aluminum foil, forming a rectangle about ½″ thick.

Mix the ingredients of the filling and spread evenly over the meat mixture. Now, carefully roll up the meat as you would a jelly roll. Bring up the top and bottom edges of the foil and fold them together tightly; the sides of the foil should be folded over to keep in the juices and the flavor.

Place the foil-wrapped roll on a flat tin in a 350° F. preheated oven for 1½ hours. At the end of the first hour, open the foil and spread away from the sides of the loaf to allow browning.

SIMPLE MEAT LOAF

1½ pounds hamburger
½ pound lean ground pork
¼ cup chopped onion
⅛ teaspoon pepper
1 medium carrot, grated*
1 medium raw potato, grated
2 eggs, beaten until lemon yellow
¾ cup condensed milk or rich milk from the top of the bottle
2 cups bread crumbs

Mix all of the ingredients in the order in which they are listed. Stir thoroughly. Press into a greased loaf tin and bake in a preheated 350° F. oven for 1 hour.

When serving, garnish with chopped parsley.

*If you have left-over cooked carrots or potatoes, these may be used instead of the raw ones.

MEAT LOAF WITH MUSHROOM SOUP

4 slices white bread with crusts removed
2 eggs, beaten to a lemon yellow
1½ pounds hamburger
¼ teaspoon salt
¼ teaspoon pepper
1 can condensed cream of mushroom soup
½ cup dried mushrooms (optional, but very nice to add)

Crumble the bread into the beaten eggs, then mix in all the rest of the ingredients in the order listed above. Spoon gently into a greased loaf tin. Place in a preheated 350° F. oven for 1 hour.

Fresh mushrooms, quartered, may be used in this recipe instead of the dried ones. If you are using the fresh ones, sauté a few to be used for a garnish around the edges of the plate when serving.

CHINESE CHOW MEIN LOAF

2 pounds hamburger
1 cup celery, cut into ¼" pieces
1 cup onion, cut into ¼" pieces
1 cup rice
1 can cream of mushroom soup
1 can cream of celery soup
¼ cup milk
½ teaspoon salt
¼ teaspoon pepper
1 #2 can chow mein noodles

Brown the hamburger in a deep skillet until it is all separated. Add the celery and onion. Cook over low heat until the onion is transparent and glazed. Meanwhile, place the rice in two cups of water and cook for 15 minutes, or until fluffy and tender. Rinse the rice in warm water, drain and add to the hamburger mixture.

Stir in the mushroom soup and celery soup. Add the milk, salt and pepper. Mix all very thoroughly. Put into a greased 1½ quart casserole; sprinkle the chow mein noodles over the top. Place in a 350° F. oven for 30 minutes. Serve with soy sauce if desired.

VEAL LOAF

2½ cups moist bread crumbs
3 eggs, beaten until lemon yellow
2 tablespoons grated onion
Juice of 1 lemon
2 teaspoons salt
½ teaspoon pepper
2 pounds ground veal
¼ pound salt pork, ground with the veal
½ cup cracker crumbs
4 strips salt pork

Add the bread crumbs to the beaten eggs; stir in the grated onion and the lemon juice. Add the salt and pepper. Mix in the ground veal and pork. Stir all very well.

Shape into an oblong loaf and place on a sheet of heavy aluminum foil. Press the cracker crumbs into the sides and over the top. Place the strips of salt pork diagonally across the loaf. Fold up the sides of the aluminum foil to retain the juices. Bake in a preheated 425° F. oven for 30 minutes. Then reduce heat to 300° F. and bake for an additional 1 hour and 30 minutes.

SELF-GLAZING MEAT LOAF

1 cup V-8 vegetable juice cocktail
3 slices bread, fresh and soft
3 eggs
1 teaspoon salt
¼ teaspoon pepper
1 tablespoon minced onion
1 pound ground chuck
½ pound ground ham
½ pound ground veal
4 tablespoons dark brown sugar
4 tablespoons cider vinegar
¼ teaspoon dry mustard
Dash of cayenne
2 tablespoons Worcestershire sauce
1 tablespoon water

Put the V-8 juice into a small saucepan and heat thoroughly. Place the bread, well broken up, into a medium-sized mixing bowl. Pour the vegetable cocktail over it. With the beaters of your mixer at low speed, beat until the bread and juice are thoroughly mixed and cooled. Then turn your mixer to its highest speed and add the eggs, one at a time. Add the salt, pepper and onion.

Now stir in the ground meat by hand. Be sure that all is thoroughly mixed. Mix the sugar, vinegar, dry mustard, cayenne, Worcestershire sauce and water together. Pour this into the bottom of a loaf tin. Form the meat mixture into a loaf and place in the tin. Bake in a 375° F. oven for 1 hour. At the end of this time, invert the loaf on an ovenproof platter and continue to bake for 30 minutes longer. The glaze which was at the bottom of the loaf will now glaze the top. If you wish, spoon the glaze over the top and sides from time to time.

MEAT LOAF WITH APPLE SAUCE

1 pound lean ground beef
¾ pound pork sausages (remove casings)
½ teaspoon sage
1 tablespoon Worcestershire sauce
½ teaspoon salt
2 cups canned apple sauce
1½ cups very dry bread crumbs
4 twists of pepper mill

Mix all of the ingredients together in the order in which they are given. Butter a loaf tin and pack them into it. Bake in a 350° F. oven for 45 minutes. This delicious meat loaf is excellent served cold in sandwiches.

LIMA BEAN, RICE AND HAMBURGER LOAF
(a good stretcher recipe)

1 pound hamburger
½ teaspoon paprika
½ cup chopped onion
½ teaspoon salt
¼ teaspoon pepper
1 tablespoon parsley flakes
1 cup rice
2 #2 cans lima beans, drained
1 cup stock, or 2 bouillon cubes dissolved in 1 cup water
1 can condensed tomato soup

Sauté the hamburger in a skillet until it loses its reddish color. Add the paprika and the chopped onion and continue to cook over low heat for 5 minutes longer. Then remove from heat.

Add the salt, pepper and parsley flakes; stir in the rice just as it comes from the package. Last, stir in the lima beans, stock and tomato soup. Take care not to break up the lima beans.

Place the mixture in a well-greased loaf tin and bake at 350° F. for 45 minutes, or until the center of the loaf is firm.

MEAT LOAF RING WITH CREAMED BEANS

½ pound ground veal
½ pound ground pork
½ pound ground ham
½ teaspoon salt
4 twists of pepper mill
2 eggs
4 tablespoons instant flour
2 tablespoons instant onion
1 can cream of mushroom soup
½ cup dry bread crumbs
1 package frozen green beans in cream sauce

Mix the ground veal, pork and ham together very well. Add the salt, pepper and eggs. Mix until all are thoroughly blended. Add the flour and the onion and stir again. Stir in the cream of mushroom soup. Grease a ring mold with butter and coat the inside with the bread crumbs. Carefully pour in the meat mixture; spread evenly with a rubber spatula.

Place in a 375° F. oven in a pan of water. Bake in the pan for 1 hour. Remove from oven and let cool for 5 minutes. Cook the green beans in a double boiler until they are thoroughly thawed and tender.

Invert the meat mold on a platter and pour the green beans into the center. Serve piping hot.

Variations:

Substitute 1 can cream of mushroom soup and 1 cup mushroom stems and pieces for the green beans.

Substitute 1 package frozen creamed peas for the green beans.

Substitute 1 package frozen cream-style corn for the green beans.

Substitute 1 can cream of celery soup plus 1 cup cooked celery for the green beans.

Substitute 1 package frozen peas and 1 can cream of celery soup for the green beans.

MEAT LOAF WITH YOGHURT

1 cup yoghurt
1 package onion soup mix
3 eggs, well beaten
¼ teaspoon pepper
1 teaspoon salt
1 tablespoon butter or margarine
1 cup soft bread crumbs (do not use crusts)
1½ pounds chopped beef

Mix the yoghurt, onion soup mix and eggs very well. Add the pepper and salt and set aside to allow the flavors to blend. Melt the butter or margarine in a large skillet. Add the chopped beef and brown evenly until all of the meat is well separated. Mix the bread crumbs with the eggs, yoghurt and onion soup.

Strain the browned meat through a sieve so that there is no fat left in it. Reserve the drippings. Add the browned meat to the other ingredients and mix very well. Use a small portion of the drippings to grease a loaf tin. Place the meat mixture in the tin and bake at 375° F. for 30 minutes, or until the center of the loaf is firm.

Invert the loaf on a hot platter and place under the broiler for 5 minutes to brown the bottom; then remove from oven.

FESTIVE MEAT LOAF #2

1 pound ground beef
1 pound ground veal
3 eggs, beaten to a lemon yellow
½ cup catsup
1 teaspoon salt
¼ teaspoon pepper
½ cup onion, chopped very fine
½ cup green pepper, chopped very fine
1 cup cracker crumbs
1 can tomato soup
¼ cup water

Mix the ground meat with the eggs, catsup, salt, pepper, onion and green pepper. Add the cracker crumbs and mix all very thoroughly. Place in a suitable loaf pan, cover tightly with aluminum foil and bake at 400° F. for 45 minutes. Then remove foil and pour the tomato soup, mixed with the water, over the loaf. Continue to bake for 15 minutes.

Invert on a heated platter and garnish with parsley sprigs. This will serve about 8.

CAULIFLOWER MEAT LOAF

1 large head cauliflower (approximately 8" in diameter) or
   two small heads
4 strips bacon, diced into ¼" pieces
1 pound ground chuck
½ teaspoon salt
4 twists of pepper mill
2 tablespoons dehydrated onion
1 cup moist bread crumbs
¾ cup milk
4 eggs, beaten until lemon yellow
Dash of paprika

Wash the cauliflower well and break it into pieces. If there
is a large core, cut it into slices. Place in cold water and bring
to a boil. When the larger stems can be pierced with a fork,
remove from heat and drain. Set aside to cool. Brown the
diced bacon in a frying pan. Remove bacon and set aside;
then brown the ground chuck in the bacon drippings. Add
the salt, pepper and dehydrated onion.

Cover the bottom of a greased loaf pan with pieces of cauliflower. Sprinkle with some of the bread crumbs. Follow this
with a layer of the ground meat. Repeat until all of the cauliflower, bread crumbs and meat are used up. Add the milk
to the eggs and mix very well. Pour this over the ingredients
in the loaf tin. Sprinkle bacon over the top.

Place in a 300° F. oven for 45 minutes, or until the egg
mixture has set like a custard. Invert on a hot platter and
garnish with paprika.

HAMBURGER PANCAKE LOAF

This is a recipe from the Ukraine region of Russia. When I first heard of it, it seemed impossible that you could make meat loaf with pancakes; but you can, and it is delicious.

1 cup flour
½ teaspoon salt
½ teaspoon baking powder
2 raw eggs
1 cup milk
1 tablespoon butter or margarine
1 pound ground chuck
1 small onion, minced
¼ teaspoon salt
½ teaspoon pepper
½ teaspoon Accent
2 hard-boiled eggs, chopped
¼ cup stock, or ¼ cup water with 1 bouillon cube dissolved in it
¼ cup buttered browned bread crumbs

Place the flour in a bowl and mix in the ½ teaspoon salt and the baking powder. Beat the raw eggs in the milk. Slowly stir the egg and milk mixture into the flour. Stir very well, then set aside for 25 minutes.

Meanwhile, melt the butter in a skillet, then place the ground meat in the skillet and fry until golden brown. Add the onion, ¼ teaspoon salt, pepper and Accent. Remove from heat and add the chopped hard-boiled eggs, then the stock. Stir, mixing all well.

Heat a griddle and place 1 tablespoon of batter for each of the pancakes on it. Brown on both sides; set the finished pancakes aside until all the batter is used up.

Place pancakes to cover the bottom of a greased loaf tin. Follow with about a half-inch layer of the meat mixture. Continue alternate layers of pancakes and meat until all is used up. You should end with pancakes on the last layer. Sprinkle the bread crumbs over all. Bake in a 350° F. oven for 20 minutes.

CHICK PEA-HAMBURGER LOAF

1 cup dried chick peas*
5 strips bacon, cut into ¼″ cubes
2 medium onions, diced
1 pound ground beef
¼ teaspoon grated nutmeg
½ teaspoon Accent
¼ teaspoon grated lemon rind
½ teaspoon salt
¼ teaspoon pepper
Juice of 1 lemon
½ cup catsup
¾ cup precooked rice
½ cup stock, or 2 bouillon cubes dissolved in ½ cup water

After having soaked the chick peas for at least 6 hours, drain them and cover with cold water. Bring them to a boil, then lower the heat and cook for at least 30 minutes, or until they can be pierced with a sharp fork. Drain and set aside to cool.

Fry the cubed bacon until it is brown and crisp. Remove bacon with a slotted spoon and set aside until later; reserve half of the bacon drippings in the skillet. Fry the onions in the bacon fat until they are glazed and transparent. Now fry the ground beef until it loses its red color. Add the grated nutmeg, Accent, lemon rind, salt and pepper. Continue to cook for 5 minutes longer and then add the lemon juice and catsup. Stir in the rice just as it comes from the package, and then add the stock.

Arrange half of the chick peas on the bottom of a greased loaf pan. Over this place the hamburger mixture. Arrange the remainder of the chick peas on top. Pour the stock over it, and place in a 350° F. oven for 35 minutes. Turn loaf onto a heated platter and sprinkle bacon cubes over the top.

* If your local grocer does not have them, they can be purchased in an international food store or one specializing in Greek, Armenian or Turkish food.

Chapter II

CASE THAT CASSEROLE

It took years for me to get my husband within ten feet of a casserole. To him a casserole meant something gooey, soupy, and totally without distinctive flavor. Even macaroni and cheese had to have the tar baked out of it before he would condescend to try a forkful of it. Hamburger Hot Pot, the first dish listed in this chapter, is the first casserole he liked enough to ask for a second helping.

Men seem to love casseroles that have some "chew" to them. Here are recipes for casseroles that have been tested by the severest critic I know—my husband.

HAMBURGER HOT POT

1 pound hamburger
1 can Spam or similar canned meat, cut into 1" x ½" pieces
1 8-ounce package medium-wide egg noodles
1 #2 can red kidney beans, drained
1 clove garlic, minced
1 cup sliced whole mushrooms or 1 cup pieces and stems
¼ cup chopped green pepper
½ teaspoon salt
5 twists of pepper mill, or ¼ teaspoon ground pepper
1 teaspoon Accent
1 cup tomato sauce
2 cups water
2 tablespoons butter

Sauté the hamburger until it is separated into pieces about the size of pecans, and slightly browned. Then combine it and all the other ingredients in a 2½-quart casserole. The noodles are put into this mixture just as they come from the package—no precooking.

Toss the ingredients to mix them thoroughly. Cover the casserole and bake in a 375° F. oven for 30 minutes. At the end of this time, remove cover from casserole. With a broad spoon or spatula, turn over the top ingredients so that they will get the benefit of the juice which has accumulated.

Bake 30 minutes longer without a cover. Stir occasionally to insure even cooking of the noodles. This is a wonderful and very nutritious one-dish meal.

CHUCK WAGON WESTERN BEAN CASSEROLE

1 pound hamburger
1 #4 can pork and beans
1 teaspoon prepared mustard
¼ teaspoon salt
¼ teaspoon pepper
1 large onion
½ cup catsup
1 tablespoon Worcestershire sauce

Sauté the hamburger until quite brown and separated. Drain off any excess fat. Add the beans and the other ingredients. Stir well, taking care not to mash up the beans in the process. Place in a 1½-quart covered casserole dish in a preheated 350° F. oven for 40 minutes.

This is an excellent picnic dish because it can be prepared ahead of time and warmed right in the casserole on the grill outdoors.

Variations:

Substitute 1 #2 can butter beans and 1 #2 can pork and beans for the #4 can of pork and beans.
Substitute 1 #2 can black-eyed peas and 1 #2 can pork and beans for the #4 can of pork and beans.
Substitute 1 #2 can chick peas and 1 #2 can pork and beans for the #4 can of pork and beans.
Substitute 1 #2 can lima beans and 1 #2 can pork and beans for the #4 can of pork and beans.
Substitute 1 #2 can pork and beans and 1 #2 can macaroni and cheese for the #4 can of pork and beans.
Substitute 1 #2 can pork and beans and 1 #2 can spaghetti for the #4 can of pork and beans.

MADRID RICE CASSEROLE

3 slices bacon, cut into ¼" pieces
½ cup onion, chopped fine
1½ pounds hamburger
¼ teaspoon thyme
¼ teaspoon sweet basil
1 #2 can tomato juice
1½ cups precooked rice
1 green pepper, cut into ¼" pieces
½ teaspoon paprika

Sauté the bacon in a skillet until slightly browned. Pour away most of the fat; add the onion and continue to sauté until the onion is slightly transparent. Add the hamburger to the onion and bacon, along with the thyme and basil. Cook for a few minutes longer, until the meat loses its reddish color. Remove from heat, and add the tomato juice. Stir in the rice just as it comes from the package. Add most of the green pepper, reserving a few pieces for later. Place the entire mixture in a 1½ quart casserole and sprinkle the paprika over the top.

Place the casserole in a 350° F. oven and bake for 35 minutes, uncovered. Five minutes before removing from the oven, sprinkle the remaining green pepper over the top for color. Serve right from the casserole used to bake in.

I usually bake a double quantity of this casserole, one for serving and one for freezing. This is a satisfying main dish for a hurry-up meal.

Variations:

Add 1 package frozen okra.
Add 1 package frozen zucchini squash.
Add 1 package frozen French-style green beans.
Omit the green pepper and use 1 8-ounce can of mushrooms.
Add 1 package frozen niblet-style corn.

EAT-MORE CASSEROLE

1 pound hamburger
½ pound elbow macaroni
1 cup chopped onion or ½ cup dehydrated onion soaked
   in ½ cup water
1 #2 can tomatoes
1 cup tomato sauce
¼ teaspoon salt
¼ teaspoon pepper
¼ teaspoon garlic powder
1 teaspoon Accent
1 can niblet-style corn with pimento, drained

Sauté the hamburger until a golden brown. Meanwhile, boil
the macaroni in slightly salted water until tender. Drain the
macaroni and combine it with the hamburger; add the onion,
tomatoes, tomato sauce, salt, pepper, garlic powder and Accent to the meat. Last, fold in the corn.

Place this mixture in a 1½-quart buttered casserole and
put into a preheated 350° F. oven; bake for 45 minutes.

If you are entertaining teen-agers with ravenous appetites,
this is a good mixture to serve on hamburger buns as "sloppy
joes." However, if you want the real "sloppy joe" recipe, it
is included in the chapter called "Shades of Lord Sandwich."

WALNUT-MEAT BALL CASSEROLE

2 pounds hamburger
1 cup chopped walnuts
1 cup bread crumbs
3 eggs, beaten to a lemon yellow
¾ cup milk
1 package dehydrated French onion soup
½ cup boiling water

Mix the hamburger, walnuts, bread crumbs, eggs and milk
thoroughly. Form into 1" diameter meat balls and brown
them a few at a time. Shaking the skillet back and forth slowly
over the flame will assure even browning.

Mix the dehydrated onion soup with the boiling water and
pour over the meat balls. Place in a preheated 350° F. oven
for a half hour. Add more water if necessary. Should you
desire additional gravy, remove meat balls, add ¾ cup of
water with tablespoon cornstarch mixed in it. Simmer for 5
minutes longer, and return meat balls to the gravy.

Variations:

Substitute 1 cup blanched Virginia peanuts for the walnuts.
Substitute 1 cup cashew nuts for the walnuts.
Substitute 1 cup pecans for the walnuts.
Substitute 1 cup pine nuts for the walnuts.

RED LETTER DAY CASSEROLE

This casserole combines meat, potatoes and other vegetables all in one dish, and is both colorful and flavorful. If your family doesn't like vegetables, it's a painless way to get them to eat them.

1 pound hamburger
8 cooked beets, peeled and coarsely chopped
8 medium-sized cooked potatoes, coarsely chopped (left-over potatoes, even hashed brown ones, are all right in this recipe)
8 cooked carrots, coarsely chopped
1 teaspoon salt
¼ teaspoon pepper
1 teaspoon Accent
2 tablespoons butter
¼ cup soup stock, or 1 bouillon cube dissolved in ¼ cup water

Sauté the ground beef until it is in pieces about the size of pecans, and slightly brown. Drain off any excess fat. To the browned meat add the chopped beets, potatoes and carrots. Add the salt, pepper and Accent. Place in a well-greased casserole. Dot the top with pieces of butter. Add the stock or bouillon. Place in a preheated 350° F. oven and bake for 35 minutes.

MEAT BALL-BEER CASSEROLE

The first time I was served this casserole, I thought the cook had flipped her lid. Beer and meat? Well, it turned out to be delicious. Try it; you too are in for a pleasant surprise. Some strange alchemy of flavors takes place that's hard to beat.

10 onions, approximately 2" in diameter
1 pound hamburger
1 egg, whipped to a lemon/yellow
½ teaspoon salt
1 teaspoon monosodium glutamate
¼ teaspoon pepper
1 tablespoon olive oil, or any good cooking oil
1 tablespoon flour
1 teaspoon dry mustard
1 teaspoon sugar
1 small bay leaf
¼ teaspoon thyme
1 12-ounce bottle beer
1 pound fresh mushrooms, or 1 #2 can mushrooms
Water cress, parsley or spinach for garnish

Peel the onions and put a toothpick through the middle of each one to prevent them from coming apart. Cover with warm water and boil until the outer shell begins to get transparent. Do not cook them completely—the final cooking takes place in the casserole. Drain and set aside to cool. Do not remove toothpicks until the onions are cool.

Mix the hamburger with the egg, salt, monosodium glutamate and pepper. In this instance, because you want a tightly held-together meat ball, knead the mixture for several minutes by hand. Form into very small meat balls, about 1" in diameter. I use the large end of my melon-ball maker to keep the meat balls uniform in size.

Heat the oil in your largest skillet; brown the meat balls by gently rolling them around in the pan. Try not to crowd them, or they will lose their shape. When all the meat balls are evenly browned, sprinkle the flour, mustard and sugar over their surface. By shaking the pan, roll the meat balls so that the flour mixture is evenly distributed.

Remove from the heat, add the bay leaf and thyme. Now pour over them the bottle of beer. Cover and set aside for approximately a half hour for all of the flavors to get acquainted. This wait is not a must, but it does improve the flavor.

In a 1½ quart casserole arrange the meat balls, mushrooms and onions (with toothpicks now removed) and pour over all the beer you have left in the skillet. Place in a 300° F. oven and bake for 35 minutes. Garnish with shredded water cress, parsley, or a few leaves of spinach, chopped fine.

RIPE OLIVE HAMBURGER CASSEROLE

1 tablespoon butter or margarine
1 pound ground chuck
2 cups dry fine egg noodles
3 quarts slightly salted water
1 cup sour cream
1 cup large-curd creamed cottage cheese
1 tablespoon dehydrated onion
1 clove garlic, chopped fine
1 teaspoon Accent
1 teaspoon Worcestershire sauce
1 drop Tabasco
1 #2 can pitted ripe olives
1 teaspoon paprika

Melt the butter or margarine in a deep skillet. Add the ground meat and cook until the reddish color disappears. Set aside. Boil the egg noodles in the water. Drain and add to the meat.

Stir in the sour cream, cottage cheese, onion, garlic, Accent, Worcestershire sauce and Tabasco. Chop the ripe olives rather coarsely and add to the meat mixture.

Put into a greased 1½-quart casserole. Bake at 350° F. for 30 minutes. Sprinkle with the paprika just before serving.

YAMBURGERS

¾ pound ground chuck
¾ pound lean ground pork
½ teaspoon salt
4 twists of pepper mill
6 rings pineapple
2 tablespoons butter
2 #2 cans yams or sweet potatoes, drained
¼ cup muscat raisins
¼ cup dried currants

Mix the ground beef and pork, salt and pepper together thoroughly. Form into six meat patties about the same size as the pineapple rings. Melt the butter in a skillet and brown the meat patties on each side. Mash the yams with a potato masher until they are quite fluffy. Add the raisins and currants and stir very well.

Butter the bottom and sides of a deep baking dish, and place the mashed yam mixture on the bottom. Cover the top with the pineapple rings, pushing each down into the mixture about a half inch. Place one hamburger patty on each of the pineapple rings. Bake in a preheated 350° F. oven for 30 minutes.

BUTTER BEAN-HAMBURGER CASSEROLE

1 #2 can butter beans or 1 cup uncooked lima beans
1 pound hamburger
¼ teaspoon pepper
½ teaspoon salt
Dash of nutmeg
1 egg, slightly beaten
2 tablespoons margarine or cooking oil
1 small can tomato paste
¼ teaspoon paprika
1 cup sour cream

If you are using uncooked lima beans, cover with water and boil until tender. Drain and set aside.

Thoroughly mix the hamburger, pepper, salt, nutmeg and egg. Form into meat balls about the size of apricots. Brown the meat balls in a skillet in the margarine or cooking oil. Add the tomato paste to the butter beans or lima beans, then stir in the paprika and sour cream. Last, add the browned meat balls, discarding any fat left in the skillet. Pour into a greased casserole and bake for 25 minutes at 350° F.

This casserole is equally good served either hot or cold.

DEER HUNTER'S PIE

1 pound hamburger

4 large boiled potatoes, peeled and sliced 1/8" thick

2 large onions, peeled and sliced 1/8" thick

3 large apples, preferably tart baking variety, sliced 1/8" thick

1 cup beef stock, or 1 cup water with 3 bouillon cubes dissolved in it

1/4 teaspoon grated nutmeg

1/4 teaspoon pepper

1/2 teaspoon salt

1/2 cup bread crumbs

Sauté the hamburger in a skillet until it is lightly browned and completely separated.

Arrange a layer of potatoes over the bottom of a 1 1/2 quart greased casserole, follow with a layer of meat, a layer of onions and a layer of apples. Repeat until you have used up all of the ingredients.

Heat the beef stock, add the nutmeg, pepper and salt. Stir well so that all of the salt is dissolved. Pour this over the casserole. Sprinkle the bread crumbs over the top, and add little dabs of butter if you like. Bake in a 350° F. oven for 50 minutes.

HAMBURGER OYSTER CASSEROLE

2 1/2 pounds hamburger

1 pint oysters (save the liquor)

1 cup dry bread crumbs

4 sprigs parsley, chopped fine

1 small onion, chopped very fine

1 teaspoon salt

1/4 teaspoon ground pepper

Fry the hamburger loosely until it is all browned, turning with a spatula during frying so that it is not broken up too much. Then add the drained oysters, and continue frying until the oyster edges curl—about 5 minutes. Set aside, and mix the liquor from the oysters with the bread crumbs, parsley and onion. Season with the salt and pepper. Add to the browned meat and oysters, tossing lightly to mix. Put into a well-greased casserole and bake at 350° F. for 45 minutes. Before removing from oven, slip under the broiler for a few seconds so the top can brown.

MEXICAN CASSEROLE

¾ pound ground chuck
¾ pound lean ground pork
2 cups cooked broad noodles
1 8-ounce can tomato sauce
2 cups American process cheese, diced into ¼" pieces
¼ cup minced parsley
3 preserved pimentos, sliced into long strips ¼" wide
1 green pepper, diced into ¼" pieces
2 cups onion, diced into ¼" pieces
½ teaspoon paprika
1 teaspoon salt
4 twists of pepper mill
4 strips bacon, diced into ¼" pieces

Mix together all of the ingredients except the diced bacon. Sprinkle the bacon over the bottom of a 1½-quart buttered casserole. Top the bacon with the meat and vegetable mixture. Bake in a 350° F. oven for 1 hour.

HAMBURGER-CABBAGE CASSEROLE

1 pound hamburger
1 tablespoon dehydrated onion
4 eggs
1 cup of milk
1 teaspoon sugar
½ teaspoon salt
¼ teaspoon pepper
1 2-pound cabbage
½ cup bread crumbs

Brown the hamburger and cook until it is all separated. Add the onion and cook for a few minutes longer. Remove from the heat. Beat the eggs until they are lemon yellow, add the milk gradually and continue beating. Add the sugar to the milk and eggs. Stir in the hamburger. Add the salt and pepper. Mix well.

Slice the cabbage very fine. Cover with water and cook for 7 minutes; drain, discarding the water. Place the boiled cabbage in a deep, greased casserole. Pour the hamburger mixture over the cabbage. Sprinkle the top with bread crumbs. Bake in a 350° F. oven for 50 minutes.

The bread crumbs should become golden brown during this cooking time. If they are not, place the casserole under the broiler for a few minutes before serving.

RAW POTATO CASSEROLE

½ pound ground chuck
½ pound lean ground pork
1 can condensed tomato soup
½ teaspoon salt
4 twists of pepper mill
1 tablespoon flour
2 tablespoons butter or margarine
1 8-ounce can mushroom stems and pieces (do not drain)
1 large onion, diced
3 cups raw potatoes, diced in ½" pieces

Mix the ground meat with the tomato soup, salt and pepper. Work in the flour. Form into meat balls about the size of golf balls. Melt the butter in a skillet and brown the meat balls on all sides.

Place the meat balls on the bottom of a well-greased 1½-quart casserole. Mix the mushrooms, onion and raw potatoes very well, and pour over the meat balls. Cover with aluminum foil and bake at 350° F. for 45 minutes. Then remove the foil and continue to bake for 15 minutes longer. Serve piping hot.

HEARTY CASSEROLE

1 tablespoon butter or margarine
½ cup chopped onion
1 pound ground chuck
½ pound American process cheese, cut into ¼" cubes
1 8-ounce package elbow macaroni, cooked in 3 quarts salted, boiling water
1 tablespoon mustard
1 package frozen corn
½ teaspoon salt
¼ teaspoon pepper
1 can condensed tomato soup

Melt the butter in a skillet, add the onion and cook until transparent. Then add the meat and continue to cook until it loses its reddish color. Set aside to cool.

Mix the cheese, macaroni, mustard, corn, salt, pepper and tomato soup. Stir in the mixture of meat and onion. Place in a 1½-quart buttered casserole and bake at 350° F. for 1 hour. Serve piping hot.

WILD RICE AND HAMBURGER CASSEROLE

¾ cup wild rice
2 cups slightly salted water
1 pound combined beef, veal and pork ground together
½ cup chopped onion
½ cup celery, chopped fine
½ teaspoon salt
½ teaspoon Accent
½ teaspoon Worcestershire sauce
1 can condensed cream of mushroom soup
¼ cup sherry wine
¼ cup grated Parmesan cheese
1 cup quartered canned or fresh mushrooms, if desired

Cook the wild rice in the water until each grain is doubled in size. Drain rice, rinse in warm tap water, and set aside in strainer to drain thoroughly dry.

Sauté the ground meat till brown, add the onion, celery, salt, Accent and Worcestershire sauce. Stir in the wild rice and mushroom soup. Add the wine. Place in a well-greased casserole; sprinkle the cheese over the top. Bake in a 350° F. oven for 1 hour.

Since wild rice and mushrooms complement each other, you may also use a cup of canned or fresh mushrooms in this recipe.

Variations:

Substitute ¼ cup grated American cheese for the Parmesan cheese.
Substitute ¼ cup feta (Greek) cheese for the Parmesan cheese.
Substitute 1 can cream of celery soup for the mushroom soup.
Substitute 1 can cream of asparagus soup for the mushroom soup.
Substitute 1 can cream of chicken soup for the mushroom soup.

EGGPLANT, LAMB AND CRACKED WHEAT CASSEROLE

3 tablespoons olive oil
1 pound ground lamb
½ cup chopped onion
½ cup chopped green pepper
1 #2 can tomatoes
1 medium-sized eggplant, peeled and cut into 1″ pieces
2 cloves garlic
1 teaspoon salt
4 twists of pepper mill
1 tablespoon lemon juice
1 teaspoon lemon rind
¾ cup cracked wheat
1 cup water
½ cup Parmesan-Romano cheese

Place 1 tablespoon of the olive oil in a skillet and brown the ground lamb. Add the onion and green pepper and cook until they are glazed and soft. Stir in the tomatoes and set aside.

Meanwhile, in another skillet, heat the remaining 2 tablespoons of olive oil and sauté the eggplant cubes until they are almost tender. Add the garlic, salt, pepper, lemon juice and rind. Cook the cracked wheat in the water until all the kernels are separated, doubled in size and tender. All of the water should be absorbed in the cooking.

Place half of the cracked wheat in the bottom of a well-buttered 2-quart casserole. Put half the lamb mixture over this, then half the eggplant, and repeat the layers with the other half of each. Sprinkle the cheese over the top and place in a 350° F. oven for 30 minutes. Serve piping hot.

You can make variations on this delicious casserole by substituting ground beef, ground ham, or a mixture of ground beef, veal and pork for the lamb.

HAMBURGER AND RICE CASSEROLE

1 pound hamburger
1 teaspoon onion juice or 1 tablespoon onion, chopped very
    fine
½ cup celery, chopped fine
¼ teaspoon ground black pepper
1 teaspoon salt
Dash of nutmeg
1 8-ounce can tomato sauce
1 egg
2 cups cooked regular rice
½ cup dry bread crumbs
1 tablespoon butter or margarine

Put the hamburger into a good-sized mixing bowl; add the
onion, celery, black pepper, salt and nutmeg. Mix all very
thoroughly; then stir in the tomato sauce.

In another mixing bowl, beat the egg with a rotary beater
until light and lemon colored. Add the rice and mix thoroughly.
Press half the rice-egg mixture around the sides and over
the bottom of a well-greased casserole. Reserve the other
half of the rice to go over the top.

Place this casserole under the broiler for 5 minutes, or
until the rice begins to brown and is set firmly around the
sides. Remove from the oven, and put in the meat mixture
carefully, using a rubber spatula to spread it evenly. Cover
with the remainder of the rice-egg mixture, and sprinkle the
bread crumbs over the top. Dot with the butter or margarine.

Bake at 350° F. for 45 minutes. Just before serving, place
under the broiler for a few seconds to brown the crumbs on
top.

Chapter III

SERVE IT IN ONE DISH

IF I CAN MAKE ONE-DISH MEALS, I generally do. To the busy housewife there is nothing more discouraging than a sinkful of cooking pots in addition to the piles of plates, knives and forks. Even if you are fortunate enough to own an automatic dishwater, washing pots is still a chore. So here are one-dish recipes I love because they save so much washing-up.

ONION HAMBURGER STEW

2 pounds hamburger
2 eggs, beaten until lemon yellow
½ cup olive oil
10 medium-sized red Italian onions (if not available, use white or yellow)
1 #2 can tomatoes
½ cup white vinegar
1 teaspoon pickling spices, tied in a little cloth sack so they can be removed
2 cloves of garlic, minced (optional)
½ teaspoon salt
¼ teaspoon pepper
½ teaspoon monosodium glutamate

Thoroughly mix the ground hamburger with the two beaten eggs. Knead by hand so that the meat balls will be very firm. With the large end of your melon-ball scoop, form 1″ diameter meat balls. Heat the olive oil in a large skillet and slowly brown the meat balls. Shake the pan in a back and forth motion to keep them round and to insure even browning.

Peel the onions and add them; continue to cook until the outer skins begin to glaze. Add the tomatoes, vinegar, spice bag, garlic, salt, pepper and monosodium glutamate. Cover and simmer for 2 hours.

If desired, you can add about 8 medium-sized potatoes 45 minutes before the dish is done. If additional water is needed, add enough to keep the stew from scorching. Remove the bag of spices before serving the stew.

STUFFED TOMATOES, ITALIAN STYLE

1 pound hamburger
4 large ripe tomatoes
½ cup precooked rice
¼ cup grated Parmesan-Romano cheese
2 tablespoons chopped parsley
2 4-inch square slices of Swiss cheese, cut into ¼" cubes
1 teaspoon monosodium glutamate
¼ teaspoon salt
¼ teaspoon pepper
¼ teaspoon sweet basil

Brown the hamburger in a skillet until it is completely separated; turn off the heat and let cool until you have the tomatoes ready. Boil the rice in 1½ cups of water until double in size; rinse and drain. Set aside to cool.

Cut off ¼" of the top of each tomato. With a teaspoon, very carefully scoop out the center pulp, leaving about a ½" wall. Add the pulp you have removed to the hamburger, and turn the heat low. Cook for 5 minutes longer, or until the tomato pulp is broken up; now add the Parmesan-Romano cheese, parsley, Swiss cheese, monosodium glutamate, salt, pepper and basil. Lastly, fold in the cooked rice.

Fill each tomato cavity with the mixture; use a teaspoon to pack it in. Place the stuffed tomatoes in a greased shallow baking dish and bake in a 350° F. oven for 35 minutes.

Care must be taken not to overcook this dish; you want the tomatoes to retain their shape, not become a mushy mess.

Variations:

Substitute grated American cheese for the Parmesan-Romano.
Substitute feta (Greek) cheese for the Parmesan-Romano.
Substitute ½" cup crushed fine egg noodles for the rice.
Add ½ cup green pepper, diced very fine.
Add ½ cup niblet-style corn.
Wrap each tomato with a slice of bacon fastened with a toothpick before putting it in the oven.

HAMBURGER CHOW MEIN

1 pound of pork, veal and beef, ground together
6 medium-sized onions cut in ¼" slices
2 cups celery, cut in ¼" slices
1 #2 can of tomatoes
1 #2 can of bean sprouts
1 #2 can of mushroom stems and pieces
1 7-ounce can water chestnuts (optional)
1 tablespoon soy sauce
1 teaspoon bead molasses
1 teaspoon monosodium glutamate
1 #2 can chow mein noodles

Slowly sauté the meat until it is in lumps about the size of hickory nuts, and light brown in color. The pork in the mixture should supply enough fat for sautéing.

Add the onions, celery and tomatoes and simmer slowly for 35 minutes. Do not cover, or celery will lose its green color. Add the bean sprouts, mushrooms, water chestnuts, soy sauce, molasses and monosodium glutamate. Simmer for 10 minutes longer. Heat the noodles in the oven at 250° F. for 10 minutes. Serve the chow mein over the heated noodles.

If you really want to show off, add about 10 sliced almonds and a few cubes of pimento to the recipe and sprinkle a little of each over the top of each serving.

Variations:

Substitute 1 10½-ounce can cream chicken soup and 1 can of water for the tomatoes.
Substitute 1 10½-ounce can cream of mushroom soup and 1 can of water for the tomatoes.
Substitute 1 10½-ounce can cream of celery soup and 1 can of water for the tomatoes.
Substitute 1 8-ounce package medium-sized egg noodles, boiled until tender, for the chow mein noodles.
Substitute 3 cups cooked rice for the chow mein noodles.
Substitute 2 packages frozen French-fried onion rings for the chow mein noodles.

ONIONS AND HAMBURGER, MILAN STYLE

4 large Bermuda onions, or 8 medium-sized onions
1 pound hamburger
8 soda crackers, soaked in enough milk to soften
¼ cup Parmesan cheese
2 3″ diameter ginger snaps, broken into small pieces
¼ teaspoon salt
¼ teaspoon pepper, or 4 twists of pepper mill
½ teaspoon monosodium glutamate
2 tablespoons chopped parsley
2 eggs, beaten until lemon yellow
½ teaspoon paprika

Very carefully peel the onions, removing only the first layer of the peeling. Cut a ½″ slice from the top of the onion —enough so that all the inner rings are exposed. Stick a toothpick into the side of the onion straight through the center. If the onions are very large, insert toothpicks from each side. This is to keep the onions from losing their shape during cooking. Place the onions in a saucepan, cover with water and boil very slowly for 20 minutes. Set them aside in their own liquid to cool so that you can handle them with ease.

Brown the hamburger in a skillet until it is all separated and in small pieces. Now remove the toothpicks from the onions and, using a teaspoon, carefully scoop out the centers. Leave about a ½″ wall. Add to the hamburger the onion centers you scooped out.

Cook the hamburger and onion centers until the onion breaks apart and is glazed. Remove from the heat and stir in the drained soda crackers. Stir in the Parmesan cheese. Next add the pieces of ginger snaps and stir until they are completely dissolved. Add the salt, pepper, monosodium glutamate and parsley. When the mixture has cooled, add half of the beaten eggs. Reserve the other half until later.

Using a teaspoon, pack the filling into each onion shell, taking care not to break through the outer walls. Place the onions in a buttered baking dish. Pour the remainder of the beaten eggs, by tablespoonfuls, over the onions. Sprinkle a little of the paprika over them. Place in a preheated 350° F. oven and bake for 35 minutes.

Variations:

Substitute ground lean pork for the hamburger.

Substitute a mixture of pork and veal for the hamburger.

Substitute a mixture of ham and hamburger for the straight hamburger.

Add ¼ teaspoon cloves and ¼ teaspoon allspice, if you like food to be spicy.

ONE-DISH MEAL

1 pound hamburger
2 onions, peeled and cut in ⅛" slices
1 teaspoon salt
¼ teaspoon pepper
3 large raw potatoes, peeled and diced into ½" pieces
3 large carrots, peeled and diced into ½" pieces
1 cup precooked rice
Water to cover

Brown the hamburger in a skillet until it loses its reddish color. Add the onions and continue to cook until they are glazed and transparent. Add the salt and pepper.

In a greased 1½-quart casserole, place the potatoes first; follow with a layer of carrots, then a layer of rice. Last, add the sautéed meat and onion mixture. Pour on enough water to cover. Leave the casserole uncovered and place in a 350° F. oven for 1 hour.

Serve hot, right from the casserole.

Variations:

Substitute 1 #2 can of peas and carrots for the raw potatoes.

Substitute 1 #2 can boiled onions for the fresh onions; leave them whole.

Substitute 1 #2 can of boiled potatoes for the fresh ones; leave them whole.

Substitute 1 #2 can corn, cream or niblet style, for the carrots.

Substitute 1 8-ounce package fine egg noodles (uncooked) for the rice.

KIDNEY BEAN SPECIAL

4 large potatoes, scrubbed, unpeeled, cut in ¼" slices
4 onions, cut in ¼" slices
1 cup precooked rice
1 pound hamburger
1 #2 can peas, drained
1 #2 can red kidney beans, not drained
1 8-ounce can tomato sauce
1 cup warm water
1 cup crushed potato chips

Butter a 1½-quart casserole and place the slices of potato in the bottom. Add a dash of salt and pepper, then a layer of onions. Next add a layer of precooked rice, as it comes from the package. Then place the raw hamburger, broken into pieces, over the rice. Salt and pepper again.

Next add the peas, then the kidney beans. Mix the tomato sauce with the water and pour over the top of the casserole. Sprinkle with the potato chips. Place in a 375° F. oven for 1½ hours. Serve piping hot.

Variations:

Substitute 1 cup dry fine noodles for the rice.
Substitute 1 cup brown rice for the white rice.
Use ½ cup wheat germ and ½ cup rice instead of all rice.
Substitute 1 #2 can pork and beans for the kidney beans.
Substitute 1 #2 can butter beans for the kidney beans.
Substitute 1 #2 can chick peas for the kidney beans.
Substitute 1 #2 can black-eyed peas for the kidney beans.
Substitute 1 #2 can niblet-style corn for the kidney beans.

HAMBURGER-FILLED ACORN SQUASH

6 tablespoons butter
2 cloves garlic, cut into very thin slices
1 pound hamburger
4 slices white bread with crusts removed
1 cup milk
1 egg, beaten to a lemon yellow
½ cup chopped parsley
½ cup chopped celery
¼ teaspoon salt
¼ teaspoon pepper
1 teaspoon monosodium glutamate
4 acorn squash, sliced lengthwise, with the seeds and pulp
   removed
⅓ cup water

Melt the butter in a skillet, being careful not to burn it.
Add the cut-up garlic and sauté for 5 minutes. Now remove
the garlic and discard it. Here garlic is used as a very subtle
flavoring agent, if left in it would overwhelm the squash flavor.

Brown the meat in the garlic-flavored butter; break up the
slices of bread and soak in the milk; to the bread mixture add
the egg, parsley, celery, salt, pepper and monosodium glutamate. Stir in the meat mixture, and continue to mix and
stir until all is very smooth.

Fill each squash half with a portion of the mixture, then
place the filled squash in a shallow baking pan. Pour the
water into the bottom of the pan. Do not cover. Place in a
preheated 350° F. oven and bake for 1 hour, or until the
sides of the squash can be pierced with a fork.

Variations:

Substitute lean ground pork for the hamburger.
Substitute lean ground ham for the hamburger.
Substitute a mixture of half pork sausage with casings re-
   moved and half hamburger for all hamburger.
Substitute a mixture of half ham and half hamburger for
   all hamburger.
Use 1 cup cooked rice in place of the bread; diminish the
   milk by half.

HAMBURGER ENCHILADAS

Meat Filling

1 pound ground chuck
1 tablespoon olive oil
½ teaspoon salt
4 twists of pepper mill
1 clove minced garlic

Sauce

1 can condensed tomato soup
¼ teaspoon garlic salt
Dash of cayenne pepper
½ cup water
Pinch oregano

Tortillas

1 cup instant flour
1 cup yellow corn meal
½ teaspoon salt
¼ cup shortening
½ cup warm milk

Vegetable Filling

½ cup chopped onion
1 cup shredded chopped lettuce
½ cup sharp American cheese

Brown the meat in olive oil. Add the salt, pepper and garlic. Set aside while you make the sauce.

Put the tomato soup, garlic salt, pepper, water and oregano in a saucepan and bring to the simmering point. It can continue simmering while you prepare the tortillas.

Mix the flour, corn meal and salt together. Cut in the shortening until it is very crumbly. Slowly add the warm milk. Mix until you have a soft dough. Knead on a lightly floured board 60 times. Divide into 10 balls and set them aside for 15 minutes, covered with a cloth. Then roll the dough into 8" rounds. Fry on a hot ungreased griddle until they start to turn brown in spots.

Dip each tortilla into the sauce until it is soft. Put a heaping tablespoonful of the meat mixture in the middle of each one. Add a little of the chopped onion, some of the lettuce and a teaspoonful of the cheese. Roll each tortilla and place it seam side down in a buttered baking dish. Pour the remainder of the sauce over the tortillas and bake in a 350° F. oven for 20 minutes.

Serve piping hot. This will serve 5 people, allowing two enchiladas for each.

MEXICAN HAMBURGER AND RICE

1 tablespoon olive oil
1 cup rice
1 pound ground chuck
1 medium onion, chopped fine
2 cloves garlic, minced
1 #2 can tomatoes
2 bouillon cubes dissolved in 1 cup warm water
1 tablespoon chili powder
1 teaspoon salt
Dash of cayenne

Heat the olive oil in a deep skillet with a tight-fitting cover. Add the rice and cook until it turns white. Add the ground meat and cook until it is golden brown. Add the onion and garlic, and cook until the onion is transparent. Add the tomatoes, bouillon, chili powder, salt and cayenne. Mix all very well.

Cover and simmer for 35 minutes, stirring from time to time. During this process all of the liquid should be absorbed by the rice. If it is not, cook for 5 minutes longer with a double thickness of dish towel between the lid and the top of the pan. The towel will absorb any additional moisture.

QUICK HAMBURGER GOULASH

2 pounds hamburger
1 cup onions, sliced
2 cups wide noodles, previously cooked
1 tablespoon dehydrated parsley
1 #2 can tomatoes
1 #2 can corn
1 teaspoon salt
4 twists of pepper mill
½ teaspoon paprika

Place the hamburger in a large skillet with a tight-fitting cover and brown the meat until it loses its reddish color. Add the onions and cook until they are transparent. Stir in the remainder of the ingredients and let simmer for about 40 minutes. Keep tightly covered all the while it is cooking.

HAMBURGER AND ZUCCHINI

2 pounds zucchini squash, unpeeled
4 slices ham, diced in ¼" pieces
3 slices bacon, diced in ¼" strips
½ cup onion. chopped
1 pound hamburger
1 tablespoon parsley flakes
½ teaspoon salt
4 twists of pepper mill
¼ cup chopped pimento, fresh or preserved

Wash the zucchini in cold water. Put in a pot with enough cold water to cover, and bring to a boil. Drain and set aside to cool. Do not cover pan while boiling zucchini, as that would make it lose its beautiful green color.

Place the ham and bacon in a skillet and fry until the bacon is a golden color. Now add the onion and fry until it is clear and glazed. Add the hamburger and fry until its red color has disappeared. Remove from heat and stir in the salt, pepper, pimento and parsley.

Cut the cooled zucchini in half and arrange in the bottom of a greased baking dish. Place the hamburger mixture over the zucchini. Bake in a 350° F. oven for 45 minutes.

HAMBURGER BAKE

2 pounds ground chuck
2 tablespoons butter or margarine
4 medium onions, sliced ¼" thick
½ cup catsup
1 tablespoon dehydrated parsley
1 tablespoon Worcestershire sauce
1 teaspoon salt
4 twists of pepper mill
1 lemon, cut into ⅛" slices

Form the meat into a huge patty about 2" thick. Place it on a piece of aluminum foil large enough to wrap the patty tightly. Melt the butter in a skillet and brown the onions in it. Place the buttered onions on top of the ground meat.

Mix the catsup, parsley, Worcestershire sauce, salt and pepper. Bring up the sides of the foil to form a border around the meat, and pour the catsup mixture over the meat and onions. Place the lemon slices on top.

Tightly seal the foil, and place meat in a 350° F. oven

for 40 minutes. Just before removing from oven, roll back the foil to form a dishlike arrangement, move the onions and lemon off to the sides and put the dish under the broiler for 5 minutes.

HAMBURGER WITH CORN MEAL BISCUITS

1 tablespoon olive oil
1 pound hamburger
1 #2 can tomatoes
4 onions, chopped very fine
1 4-ounce can mushroom stems and pieces
½ cup catsup
½ cup water
½ teaspoon salt
¼ teaspoon sweet basil
3 green peppers, chopped

Biscuits

1 cup yellow corn meal
1 cup instant or all-purpose flour
1 teaspoon salt
1 tablespoon baking powder
¼ cup shortening
¾ cup milk

Heat the olive oil in a skillet, add the hamburger and cook until all the reddish color disappears. Add the tomatoes, onions and mushrooms. Mix the catsup with the water and add to the meat mixture. Add the salt, basil and green peppers. Place the mixture in a well-greased 1½-quart casserole.

Mix the corn meal, flour, baking powder and salt together. Cut in the shortening. Blend until the mixture is crumbly. Slowly add the milk. Mix until a soft dough is formed. Turn out on a lightly floured board and knead 20 times. Roll out the dough until it is ½″ thick. Cut into 3″ circles. Arrange the circles on top of the meat mixture.

Place the casserole in a 400° F. oven for 15 minutes, or until the biscuits are golden brown. Serve hot. This dish will serve 6.

MEAT BALLS, MACARONI AND BROCCOLI

1 pound hamburger
¼ teaspoon oregano
½ teaspoon salt
4 twists of pepper mill
Pinch of thyme
¼ cup olive oil
1 pound elbow macaroni
1 pound broccoli
½ cup Parmesan cheese

Mix the hamburger meat with the oregano, salt, pepper and thyme. Form into meat balls about the size of golf balls. Sauté until golden brown in 2 tablespoons of the olive oil.

Boil the elbow macaroni until it is tender. Rinse in tepid water and set aside. Clean the broccoli under running water. Break apart the blossoms, and cut the stalks into ¼" slices. Boil for 8 minutes in salted water. Drain.

Put the remainder of the olive oil into a large baking dish. Swirl it around so that the bottom and sides are completely covered. Place the macaroni in the bottom of the baking dish. Add the meat balls, and sprinkle with half of the cheese. Put the broccoli over this and sprinkle the remainder of the cheese over the top.

Bake in a 350° F. oven for 20 minutes. Serve piping hot.

HAMBURGER, HERBS AND RICE

1 pound hamburger
2 tablespoons butter
2 tablespoons dehydrated onion
½ cup chopped celery
¼ cup chopped parsley
¼ teaspoon salt
¼ teaspoon pepper
1 #2 can chicken broth
2 cups precooked rice
⅛ teaspoon oregano
Pinch of thyme
Pinch of rosemary
Pinch of marjoram

Sauté the hamburger in the butter until well separated and slightly browned. Add the onion, celery and parsley, and cook for 5 minutes longer. Add the salt, pepper and chicken broth. Stir in the rice and herbs. Cook over very low heat, covered, for 15 minutes, or until the rice is tender.

Serve garnished with a little additional parsley.

CABBAGE LEAVES STUFFED WITH HAMBURGER

1 medium-sized white cabbage
1 pound hamburger
2 tablespoons butter or margarine for browning meat
1 large onion, chopped very fine
1 cup precooked rice
2 tablespoons butter or margarine for browning cabbage rolls
1 tablespoon flour
1 10-ounce can beef consommé or 1½ cups of beef stock
1 cup sour cream
½ teaspoon salt
¼ teaspoon pepper
Juice of lemon
1 cup canned tomatoes or 1 cup chopped fresh tomatoes

Clean the cabbage by removing the tough outer leaves and rinsing under cold running water. Place the whole cabbage in a large kettle of slightly salted water. Bring to a boil, then reduce heat to a simmer until the outer leaves of the cabbage begin to pull away easily. Remove it from the water, let drain and cool. Discard the water it was boiled in.

Brown the hamburger in the butter or margarine. Add the onion to the meat and continue to cook until the onion is transparent. Remove from the heat and stir in the rice just as it comes from the package.

Carefully remove the cabbage leaves from the head, using a sharp knife to cut them off from the core or heart. In the center of each leaf place a tablespoonful of the meat and rice mixture. Fold the leaf around very tightly and fasten with a toothpick. Melt the butter or margarine and brown the cabbage rolls on all sides. When browned, place in a casserole in layers.

To the butter you have left after browning the cabbage rolls, add the flour. Brown the flour and then add the consommé or stock; cook until slightly thickened. Remove from the heat; stir in the sour cream, add the salt and pepper; add the lemon juice and tomatoes. Blend all well and pour over the cabbage rolls. Bake in a 350° F. oven for 45 minutes.

HAMBURGER PATTIES IN HORSE-RADISH AND SOUR CREAM SAUCE

1 pound ground beef
½ pound ground pork
1 large onion, grated or minced
1 clove garlic, chopped very fine
2 tablespoons dehydrated parsley flakes
2 shredded wheat biscuits, rolled very fine
1 egg
1 teaspoon salt
4 twists of pepper mill
¼ cup Parmesan-Romano cheese

Sauce

2 tablespoons butter
2 tablespoons horse-radish, thoroughly drained
2 beef bouillon cubes
1 cup warm water
1 tablespoon cornstarch
2 tablespoons cider vinegar
1 cup sour cream

Mix the beef, pork, onion, garlic, parsley flakes and shredded wheat biscuits together. Add the egg, salt, pepper and cheese. Again mix very thoroughly. Form into 3″ round patties and brown on both sides in the butter. Remove the patties from the skillet and set aside.

In the butter which remains in the skillet, brown the horse-radish for a few seconds. Dissolve the bouillon cubes in the warm water and then stir in the cornstarch. Add this bouillon-cornstarch mixture to the horse-radish. Cook for 5 minutes, or until slightly thickened, and then add the vinegar. Remove from the heat and slowly stir in the sour cream. Put the hamburger patties in the sour cream-bouillon mixture, and cook very slowly for an additional 15 minutes.

This is a good dish to prepare ahead of time, as it can be rewarmed without losing its flavor.

CURLY KALE AND HAMBURGER

2 pounds curly kale
6 medium-sized potatoes, peeled and quartered
4 tablespoons dry quick-cooking oatmeal
1 can bouillon or 1½ cups soup stock
½ teaspoon salt
¼ teaspoon pepper
1 pound hamburger
2 tablespoons butter or margarine

Place the kale, potatoes, oatmeal and bouillon in a sauce-pan and cook for approximately 15 minutes. Turn frequently so that all of the kale is thoroughly cooked. Mix the salt and pepper with the hamburger and form into little meat balls; brown in the butter or margarine.

Mash the kale-potato mixture thoroughly, place on a platter and garnish with the browned meat balls.

HAMBURGER-HAM AND ORANGES

1 pound hamburger
½ pound ground lean ham
½ teaspoon salt
¼ teaspoon pepper, or 4 twists of pepper mill
1 egg
1 cup soft bread crumbs
1 teaspoon prepared yellow mustard
½ cup milk
4 large oranges, peeled
½ cup catsup
¼ cup brown sugar

Mix the hamburger with the lean ham. Add the salt, pepper, egg, bread crumbs, mustard and milk. Mix all very well. Form into eight patties about ¾" thick and 3" in diameter.

Cut the round ends off each orange. Slice each orange in half so that you end up with 8 generous slices. Place the orange halves in a flat baking dish. Mix the catsup and brown sugar together and put a generous tablespoonful of the mixture on top of each orange. Place the meat patties on top of this.

Bake in a 350° F. oven for 1 hour. Ten minutes before serving, carefully turn over each patty and orange half so that the meat can absorb the juice in the bottom of the pan. Serve with the orange slice up. Garnish with parsley, if desired, for additional color.

ONIONS STUFFED WITH HAMBURGER

10 yellow onions approximately 2-3" in diameter
1 cup cooked regular rice
½ cup condensed milk
1 pound hamburger
1 egg, slightly beaten
1 teaspoon salt
¼ teaspoon pepper
1 tablespoon butter or margarine
2 tablespoons lemon juice

Cut off the stem ends of the onions to a depth of ½"; pare the root end just enough to remove the roots. Then peel each onion carefully, making sure that the outside first layer is completely intact. Put the onions in a kettle and cover with salted water; boil for 10 minutes, or until the outer three layers of each onion can be pricked easily with a toothpick.

Meanwhile, simmer the cooked rice in the condensed milk until it is thick and the consistency of rice pudding. Set aside to cool. When cool, mix with the meat and egg. Add the salt and pepper.

Drain the cooked onions, reserving ½ cup of the liquid. With a teaspoon, scoop out the centers of the onions and replace with the meat mixture, packing as firmly as possible. Place the stuffed onions in a casserole dish, using the center portions to fill in between the stuffed onions. Heat the half cup of onion liquid in a saucepan, add the butter and the lemon juice. When hot, pour over the onions. Then place the casserole in a 350° F. oven for 30 minutes.

LITTLE MEAT LOAVES

¾ pound ground chuck
¾ pound ground ham
1 cup left-over or instant mashed potatoes
3 eggs, beaten to a golden yellow
½ cup condensed milk
1 cup dry bread crumbs or 1 cup crushed Wheaties
1 teaspoon salt
4 twists of pepper mill
1 cup water with 2 bouillon cubes dissolved in it

Mix the chuck, ham and mashed potatoes. Add the eggs and milk. Work in the bread crumbs or Wheaties. Add the salt and pepper.

Form into little loaves about 3″ long and 2″ wide. Place them in rows in a buttered coffee-cake tin. Add the water with the bouillon cubes in it. Cover the tin with aluminum foil.

Place in a 375° F. oven for 1 hour. Just before serving, remove the foil and brown the tops of the loaves under the broiler.

STEAK AND POTATOES

2 pounds ground beef (preferably chuck)
½ cup powdered dry milk
1 teaspoon salt
¼ teaspoon pepper
1 egg
¾ cup soft bread crumbs
4 or 5 potatoes, baked or boiled
1 large onion
1 large green pepper
1 teaspoon prepared mustard
1 tablespoon Worcestershire sauce
2 cups tomato juice
6 tablespoons grated Parmesan cheese

Thoroughly mix hamburger, milk, salt, pepper, egg and bread crumbs. Form into six large patties approximately 4″ in diameter. Brown the patties in a skillet and then pour away any excess grease. Place patties in a large rectangular baking dish. Cut the potatoes in half and arrange around the patties. On the top of each patty place several rings of onion and several rings of green pepper.

Mix the mustard and Worcestershire sauce with the tomato juice. Pour around the meat patties and the potatoes. Cover with aluminum foil and place in a 350° F. oven for 30 minutes. Then remove the foil and place a tablespoonful of cheese on top of each patty. Place under broiler for 5 minutes longer before serving.

Chapter IV
SHADES OF LORD SANDWICH!

BACK IN THE 17TH CENTURY, the fourth Earl of Sandwich was so involved in a hot card game that he did not want to stop to eat. So he demanded his roast beef between two slices of bread—and this, according to history, is the way the sandwich was born.

How the American hamburger evolved from that, we'll never know. However, here is a chapter loaded with variations on Lord Sandwich's idea. Hamburgers between buns have found an honored place in America. This chapter is going to be longer than the rest, for we have what is probably the largest collection of hamburger sandwich recipes in captivity!

A GOOD BASIC HAMBURGER

(to pan fry, foil wrap, or grill outdoors)

1 pound hamburger
1 teaspoon salt
4 twists of pepper mill
1 tablespoon grated onion
1 tablespoon minced parsley
½ teaspoon sugar
1 tablespoon salad oil, if hamburger is very lean
4 or 6 hamburger buns
4 to 6 tablespoons soft butter for buns

Mix together, in the order in which they are listed, all of the ingredients for the hamburger mixture. Form into 4 generous or 6 smaller patties, and brown in a skillet. Serve on the buns, after spreading them with the soft butter.

TEN VARIATIONS FOR THE BASIC HAMBURGER

Cashew Burgers

Add ¾ cup chopped salted cashew nuts to the hamburger mixture.

Pecan Burgers

Add ¾ cup chopped pecans to the hamburger mixture.

Walnut Burgers

Add ¾ cup chopped walnuts to the hamburger mixture.

Zippy Burgers

Add ½ cup chili sauce and ½ teaspoon cinnamon to the hamburger mixture.

Stretch-that-Meat Burgers

Add ¾ cup mashed potatoes and 1 well-beaten egg to the hamburger mixture.

Cheesits

Add 8 slices American process cheese, diced into ¼″ cubes, to the hamburger mixture.

Italian Burgers

Add 2 cloves minced garlic or 1 tablespoon garlic juice, and ½ cup Parmesan cheese, to hamburger mixture.

Hungarian Burgers

Add 1 large grated carrot to the hamburger mixture, and sprinkle generously with paprika before browning.

Herb Burgers

Add ¼ teaspoon thyme, ¼ teaspoon rosemary and ¼ teaspoon oregano to the hamburger mixture.

Indian Burgers

Add ⅛ teaspoon curry powder and ⅛ teaspoon corriander to the hamburger mixture.

TWENTY-FIVE GARNISHES FOR THE
BASIC HAMBURGER

After you have made the hamburgers according to the basic recipe, and put them on the buttered buns, prepare any of the following garnishes and spread them on the hamburgers while the meat is still hot:

1. Soften 4 tablespoons of butter and mix with 4 tablespoons of Heinz 57 Sauce or A-1 Steak Sauce.

2. Chop 4 sweet-sour pickles very fine. Add 4 tablespoons mayonnaise and beat together.

3. Mix together very thoroughly: 2 tomatoes, chopped very fine; ½ teaspoon sweet basil and 3 tablespoons soft butter.

4. Mix to spreading consistency: 1 4-ounce package cream cheese, softened; ¼ teaspoon thyme; ¼ teaspoon oregano and ¼ teaspoon sage.

5. Mix together 4 tablespoons softened butter, 2 tablespoons grated onion and 1 tablespoon mayonnaise.

6. Mix to spreading consistency: 4 tablespoons softened butter and 4 tablespoons pine nuts, chopped very fine.

7. Mix to spreading consistency: 4 tablespoons softened butter and 4 ounces feta (Greek) cheese.

8. Mix together ½ cup catsup; ¼ cup green pepper, chopped very fine and 1 pimento, chopped fine.

9. Mix to spreading consistency: 1 4-ounce package cream cheese, 4 tablespoons Bleu cheese and 1 tablespoon mayonnaise.

10. Mash 1 medium-sized avocado, then add to it 1 tablespoon lemon juice and a dash of Tabasco.

11. Mash 1 medium-sized avocado, then add to it 2 tablespoons lime juice, ½ teaspoon grated lime rind and a dash of cayenne.

12. Whip to spreading consistency: ¾ cup Cheese Whiz, 1 tablespoon onion juice and 1 tablespoon lemon juice.

13. Whip together to spreading consistency: ¾ cup Cheese Whiz and ¾ cup French-fried onions, crumbled.

14. Mix together ¾ cup Cheese Whiz and 5 strips of bacon, fried crisp, broken into small pieces.

15. Beat together: 4 tablespoons softened butter, 1 tablespoon bead molasses and 1 tablespoon soy sauce.

16. Place ¼"-thick slices of onions on burgers when nearly done, and brush three or four times with the following, all mixed together: 1 tablespoon sugar, 1 teaspoon salt, 1 teaspoon mustard, ½ teaspoon celery seed, ½ cup olive oil and juice of 1 large lemon.

17. Put in a saucepan and let simmer for 15 minutes: 1 cup pitted tart pie cherries, juice of 1 lemon, 1 tablespoon sugar, ½ teaspoon cinnamon and ¼ teaspoon ground cloves.

18. Put in a jar: 1 cup evaporated milk, ½ cup sugar, 2 tablespoons dry mustard, 2 tablespoons cornstarch, 1 teaspoon Accent, ½ teaspoon salt and ¼ teaspoon pepper. Shake all the ingredients together in the jar; then put them in a saucepan and cook over low heat until thick.

19. Blend together: ½ cup horse-radish, grated; 1 cup thick sour cream; 1 teaspoon sugar; ½ teaspoon salt and ¼ teaspoon pepper.

20. Melt ¾ cup Cheese Whiz in a double boiler. Add 1 small can mushroom stems and pieces, drained and chopped fine. Stir mushrooms and cheese together well.

21. Whip together until of spreading consistency: 4 tablespoons soft butter, ½ teaspoon dill seed and ½ teaspoon celery seed.

22. Put in a fruit jar: 2 tablespoons fresh dill, chopped very fine; 1 cup water; 2 beef bouillon cubes; 1 tablespoon flour; ½ teaspoon cider vinegar and 1 egg yolk. Shake all the ingredients together in the jar, then put in a saucepan and cook over low heat until thickened. Add 1 tablespoon butter. Spread over burgers and serve immediately.

23. Whip together: ½ cup mayonnaise, 1 tablespoon lemon juice and 1 tablespoon capers, crushed.

24. Mix together: 1 cup mushrooms (fresh ones, preferably), chopped very fine; ¼ cup Heinz 57 Sauce and ¼ cup mayonnaise.

25. Mix well 1 small can deviled ham; ¾ cup Virginia peanuts, chopped fine; ¼ cup sweet pickle relish and ¾ cup mayonnaise.

SESAME BURGERS

1 pound hamburger
¼ cup onion, chopped fine
1 egg, slightly beaten
¼ teaspoon nutmeg
½ teaspoon salt
4 twists of pepper mill
½ cup sesame seeds
2 tablespoons butter or margarine
4 hamburger buns

Mix the hamburger with the onion, egg, nutmeg, salt and pepper. Dipping your hands into cold water, form the mixture into 4 generous patties. Press a teaspoon of sesame seeds into each side of the raw hamburgers.

Melt the butter or margarine in a skillet and brown the hamburgers on each side. Place the hamburgers in the buns and put into the oven at 350° F. for 5 minutes.

LAMBURGERS

Ground lamb is a wonderful source of protein. When you buy it, look for lamb which is a rich reddish color; the lighter it is in color, the more fatty it is—and, naturally, the less nutritional value it contains.

1 pound ground lamb
2 cloves garlic, minced very fine, or 1 tablespoon garlic juice
1 teaspoon salt
¼ teaspoon pepper
1 tablespoon dehydrated parsley
4 tablespoons grated Parmesan cheese
4 hamburger buns

Mix the lamb with the garlic, salt, pepper and parsley. Form into 4 generous patties and place in a skillet over low heat. Fry the patties until they are golden brown. Place each patty on the bottom half of a hamburger bun; top the lamb with a tablespoonful of the cheese. Put under the broiler for 5 minutes, or until the cheese starts to bubble. Put the tops of the buns in place and serve piping hot.

Lamb is one meat which should be served hot, especially if it is ground; otherwise it loses a lot of its wonderful flavor.

GLAZED BURGERS

1 pound hamburger
1 tablespoon minced onion
1 tablespoon minced parsley
1 can dehydrated mushroom soup
1 egg, beaten until lemon yellow
2 tablespoons butter or margarine

Glaze

1 cup apple butter
1 tablespoon grated orange rind

Mix the hamburger with the onion, parsley, mushroom soup and egg. Form into 8 patties. Melt the butter or margarine in a skillet and brown the patties well on each side.

To make the glaze, put the apple butter and orange rind in the skillet. Simmer for 15 minutes, turning each patty several times so it will be well covered with the glaze.

Serve on hot hamburger buns.

BURGERS IN FOIL

1 pound hamburger
½ teaspoon salt
4 twists of pepper mill
1 tablespoon Worcestershire sauce
1 tablespoon catsup
¼ pound butter or margarine
⅛ teaspoon thyme
10-15 dill seeds
1 teaspoon soy sauce
8 hamburger buns

Mix the hamburger, salt, pepper, Worcestershire sauce and catsup very well. Form into 8 patties. Broil on each side enough to brown. Melt the butter or margarine, add the thyme, dill seeds and soy sauce. Brush the bottoms and tops of the hamburger buns generously with the flavored butter. Place a meat patty in each bun. Wrap tightly in squares of aluminum foil. Place in a 350° F. oven for 30 minutes. If onions on hamburgers are a favorite, put a large onion slice on each burger before placing in the bun.

These burgers are equally good served on an outdoor grill. All ingredients can be prepared ahead of time, and then heated around the edge of the grill while corn or potatoes are roasting.

UPSIDE-DOWN SANDWICHES

½ cup bread crumbs
1 tablespoon dehydrated onion
½ cup milk
1 pound ground beef
1 egg, beaten to a lemon yellow
2 tablespoons capers, chopped very fine
4 tablespoons butter or margarine
6 slices white bread

Place the bread crumbs and onion in the milk and let the crumbs swell and absorb all of the milk. Place the meat in a bowl and mix with the bread crumbs and milk. Add the egg and the chopped capers. Mix all very well.

Melt the butter in a skillet and place each slice of bread in it until it is golden brown on one side. Spread a generous portion of the meat mixture on the unbrowned side of the bread. Place the bread, meat side down, in the skillet and cook until the meat is browned. Serve piping hot.

BLEU CHEESE BURGERS

1 pound ground chuck
1 medium onion, chopped very fine
1 tablespoon Worcestershire sauce
1 teaspoon sugar
½ teaspoon Accent
1 teaspoon prepared mustard
¼ cup tomato sauce or ¼ cup chili sauce
6 hamburger buns
6 tablespoons soft butter or margarine
½ cup Bleu cheese mixed in ½ cup mayonnaise

Mix the ground meat, onion, Worcestershire sauce, sugar, Accent, mustard and tomato sauce very thoroughly. Set aside to allow the flavors to blend. This meat mixture can be made several hours before serving, or even the day before.

Butter the hamburger bun halves and place under the broiler until they are toasted a golden brown.

Place 1 heaping tablespoonful of the cheese and mayonnaise mixture in the center of each bun half. Form the meat into ½" thick patties the size of the buns; place the meat patty over the Bleu cheese mixture. Press the edges of each patty so that the cheese mixture is completely sealed inside. Put under the broiler for 15 minutes, or until the meat is completely browned. Serve piping hot.

This will yield 12 half buns, or 2 portions per person.

TEEN-AGERS' SPECIAL SANDWICHES

1 tablespoon dehydrated onion
2 tablespoons water
¼ teaspoon nutmeg
½ teaspoon salt
¼ teaspoon pepper
¼ teaspoon cardamon
1 pound ground round steak or very lean ground chuck
10 slices white bread
4 tablespoons butter or margarine
2 eggs
¼ cup milk

Place the dehydrated onion in the water for 10 minutes. Then mix it very thoroughly with the nutmeg, salt, pepper, cardamon and meat. Spread the meat mixture on one side of each of 5 slices of bread. Press the remaining 5 slices of bread tightly over the meat mixture.

Melt the butter or margarine in a large skillet. Meanwhile, beat the egg in the milk. Dip the sandwiches in the beaten egg mixture and then put the sandwiches in the skillet and fry slowly until each side is browned. Serve with pickle slices.

TEENS' RIB LINERS

1 pound hamburger
1 tablespoon butter or margarine
1 teaspoon salt
½ teaspoon pepper
¼ cup chopped onion
2 cloves of garlic, minced
1 #2 can red kidney beans, drained and chopped very fine
½ teaspoon oregano
½ teaspoon chili powder
8 hamburger buns

Brown the hamburger in the butter or margarine, add the salt, pepper, onion and garlic. Stir in the kidney beans. Add the oregano and the chili powder and simmer for 10 minutes longer. Put a generous spoonful of this mixture on each bun and serve with potato chips and pickles.

This is an ideal teen-age treat because it can be kept warm in the top of a double boiler and served whenever needed. This is also a good item to freeze. You can double or even triple the recipe and freeze the extra portions against that day when you are suddenly invaded by a tribe of hungry youngsters.

SLOPPY JOE

There are many versions of "Sloppy Joe" sandwiches, but the following three recipes are our favorites. Once you get the knack of making this teen-agers' delight, you will think of many variations. Sloppy Joes take only a short time to prepare, and being a mother who knows what to serve while the Beatles are bleating will mark you as "cool" forever.

2 pounds hamburger
1 large onion, diced
½ cup catsup
1 cup water
1 7-ounce can mushroom stems and pieces, drained
½ teaspoon salt
¼ teaspoon pepper
1 10½-ounce can minestrone soup
8 hamburger buns

Brown the hamburger and break it apart until it is quite fine. Add the onion and continue to cook until the onion is transparent and glazed. Add the catsup, water, mushrooms, salt, pepper and soup. Cook over low heat for 25 minutes. Stir from time to time to prevent scorching.

Place heaping spoonfuls in the middle of each hamburger bun and serve.

SLOPPIER JOES

2 pounds hamburger
1 large onion, diced
1 #2 can tomatoes
8 hamburger buns
6 slices bacon, diced and fried crisp
½ cup grated American cheese

Brown the hamburger until it is all broken apart; add the diced onion and cook until it is glazed. Add the tomatoes and simmer for 25 minutes without a cover. Stir from time to time to prevent scorching.

Remove from heat and place a heaping spoonful of the meat mixture on the bottom of each hamburger bun. (Set aside the tops temporarily.) Sprinkle with the crisp bacon, then top with the grated cheese. Place under the broiler until the cheese is melted. Cover with bun tops, and serve.

SLOPPIEST JOES

2 pounds hamburger
Dash of nutmeg
½ teaspoon salt
¼ teaspoon pepper
1 cup fresh mushrooms, cut into quarters
1 can cream of mushroom soup
1 package frozen French-fried onion rings
8 hamburger buns

Brown the hamburger until it is all broken apart. Add the nutmeg, salt and pepper. Add the mushrooms and cook for 8 minutes longer. Toss frequently during this time so that the mushrooms are warmed through. Add the soup and continue to cook for 10 minutes longer.

Place the onion rings in a 350° F. oven for 10 minutes, or until warmed through. Then place 3 or 4 onion rings on each bun bottom; top this with a heaping spoonful of the hamburger mixture. Place an additional 3 or 4 rings on top of the hamburger mixture. Put under the broiler for 5 minutes, then cover with tops of buns and serve.

SCHNITZEL BURGERS

6 tablespoons butter
2 tablespoons instant flour
1 tablespoon parsley flakes
½ teaspoon salt
4 twists of pepper mill
Pinch of mace
3 tablespoons water
1 pound ground veal
6 eggs

Melt half the butter in a saucepan over low heat. Stir in flour, parsley flakes, salt, pepper and mace. When the flour begins to brown, add the water. Cook until thickened, and then set aside to cool.

When the above mixture is cool, add the ground veal and mix very thoroughly. Form into 6 patties about 3″ in diameter. Melt the rest of the butter in a skillet and brown the patties on one side. Turn them carefully and make an indentation in each one large enough to hold an egg. Carefully break the eggs and place one in each of the indentations you have made. Cover pan tightly and cook for 20 minutes.

Serve on hot hamburger buns.

SPANISH SLOPPY JOES

1 tablespoon butter or margarine
1 pound ground chuck
1 tablespoon vinegar
1 tablespoon lemon juice
1 tablespoon Worcestershire sauce
1 cup celery, chopped very fine
1 cup onion, chopped fine
1 cup tomato catsup
1 can condensed tomato soup
1 tablespoon sugar
1 teaspoon garlic juice
1 teaspoon salt
½ cup water
4 hamburger buns

Place the butter or margarine in a deep skillet with a tight-fitting cover. Add the meat and sauté until the reddish color disappears. Stir in the vinegar and the lemon juice. Add the Worcestershire sauce, celery, onion and catsup. Bring to a simmer, and add the tomato soup. Add the sugar, garlic juice, salt and water. Cover and simmer for 1 hour.

At the end of this time the meat mixture should be thick enough to spoon onto the buns. If it is not, continue to simmer for a few minutes longer without the cover.

SPANISH HAMBURGERS

¾ pound ground beef
½ pound ground ham
½ teaspoon monosodium glutamate
2 tablespoons butter
3 tablespoons flour
3 tablespoons grated onion
1 tablespoon dehydrated parsley
1 sweet pepper (red or yellow)
1 small bay leaf, broken into tiny pieces
¼ teaspoon grated nutmeg
¼ teaspoon ground cloves
1 10½-ounce consommé, or 1¼ cups rich stock
1 cup canned tomatoes
½ cup light sherry wine

Mix the beef and the ham with the monosodium glutamate; set aside while you make the sauce, as follows:

Melt the butter in a skillet and stir in the flour. Let the mixture get slightly browned. Add the onion, parsley, sweet pepper, bay leaf, nutmeg, cloves and consommé or stock. Cook for 5 minutes or until the sauce is slightly thickened. Add the beef-ham mixture and continue to cook over low heat for 1 hour. Stir from time to time during this period to break up the ham and beef.

Then stir in the tomatoes and wine. Simmer for 5 minutes longer. Serve like Sloppy Joes on hamburger buns, or pour over boiled rice, spaghetti or macaroni.

HAMBURGERS MADE WITH WINE

1 pound ground chuck
1 pound lean ground pork
2 eggs, beaten to a lemon yellow
3 tablespoons melted butter (reserve one tablespoonful for browning patties)
½ teaspoon salt
¼ teaspoon pepper
Juice of 1 lemon
1 tablespoon grated lemon rind
3 tablespoons dehydrated onion
3 tablespoons dehydrated parsley
1 cup soft bread crumbs
½ cup light sherry wine
8 hamburger buns

Thoroughly mix the ground chuck and the ground pork; add the eggs, 2 tablespoons of melted butter, salt and pepper. Mix again, and then add the lemon juice and rind. Add the onion, parsley and bread crumbs. Mix all very thoroughly. Form into 8 patties about 1″ thick.

In the remaining tablespoonful of butter, brown the patties on both sides. Lower the heat to simmer and then add the wine. Cook over very low heat for 30 minutes. Turn the patties frequently during the cooking time so that the wine flavor penetrates the entire patty. Serve on warmed hamburger buns.

SORBONNE SANDWICHES

¾ pound ground round steak
2 egg yolks, beaten until lemon yellow
1 small onion, chopped very fine
1 medium boiled potato, chopped very fine
3 pickled beets, chopped rather coarsely
10 capers, chopped fine
½ teaspoon salt
4 tablespoons soft butter for spreading
6-8 slices bread
4 tablespoons butter or margarine for frying

Mix the meat, egg yolks, onion, potato, pickled beets, capers and salt very thoroughly. Set aside for 20 minutes to let the flavors blend.

Butter 6 to 8 slices of bread (depending on how thick your family likes the meat spread). Heat some of the butter in a skillet, and fry one side of the bread until golden brown. Spread the unbrowned side with the meat mixture and fry until brown. Serve piping hot.

If you want these sandwiches to be especially festive use circles cut out of the center of very fresh bread slices. Save the crusts for crumbs or croutons.

QUICK-AND-EASY PIZZA SANDWICHES

1 pound ground chuck
½ teaspoon salt
½ cup chili sauce
Pinch of oregano
4 English muffins
1 medium onion, sliced very thin
8 slices sharp process American cheese

Mix the ground chuck, salt, chili sauce and oregano together lightly. Split the English muffins in half. On each half, spread the meat mixture about ½" thick. Place several slices of onion on top of meat. Cut the pieces of cheese in half and crisscross them on top of the meat and onion mixture.

Place in a 400° F. oven for 8 to 10 minutes, or until the cheese is melted and bubbling. Serve immediately.

Chapter V

YOU'RE IN THE DOUGH

FOR CENTURIES, in those countries where fresh meat was scarce or there wasn't enough refrigeration to keep a supply on hand, homemakers have been dreaming up ways to make a little ground meat go a long way.

Since then we have learned that a protein-rich diet is good for us. However, many of these "stretch the meat" recipes are too delicious to pass up. Besides, in this day of high prices, high taxes, high everything, one is sometimes forced to stretch the meat.

Try these recipes at times when there is too much month left at the end of the money.

HAMBURGER PASTIES

The origin of pasties is variously attributed to the Cornish, Welsh, French, Irish, Swedes. In fact, so many people got into the act of taking credit for them, it's hard to tell exactly where they did start. But whatever their origin, the important thing is that pasties are a wonderful food, both filling and nourishing.

¾ pound hamburger
3 medium-sized cooked potatoes, diced in ½" cubes
1 onion, chopped finely, or ¼ cup dehydrated onion flakes
2 coarsely chopped cooked carrots
1 teaspoon salt
1 teaspoon pepper

Dough

1¾ cups sifted all-purpose flour
1 teaspoon baking powder
¼ teaspoon salt
6 tablespoons shortening
6 tablespoons cold water

Lightly sauté the ground meat until it is browned and about the size of hickory nuts. Add the diced potatoes, onion and carrots. (If you have bits of left-over peas, lima beans or other vegetables in the refrigerator, add them too. Anything goes in a pastie.) Add the salt and pepper and set aside to cool slightly.

Mix the flour, baking powder and salt together. Cut in the shortening with two knives or a pastry blender until it is the consistency of pie dough. Add the cold water, 1 tablespoonful at a time, and knead into a dough.

Place the dough on a floured board and roll out until it is about ¼" thick. Cut into squares or circles about 3" in diameter. On half of each square or circle, place 1 heaping tablespoonful of the meat mixture. Wet one edge of the square or circle, and bring the other half down over the meat mixture. Press the edges together. You wet the edge of the dough to insure its staying together.

Place the filled circles or squares on a greased and floured cookie sheet and bake in a 325° F. oven for 1 hour, or until the tops are golden brown.

Variations (if you have not already included left-over vegetables)

Add ¾ cup canned peas.
Add ¾ cup butter beans.
Add ¾ cup lima beans.
Add 1 coarsely chopped tomato.
Add ¾ cup cooked navy beans.
Add ¾ cup niblet-style corn.

BRITISH TOADS

½ pound ground beef
½ pound ground pork
¼ teaspoon pepper
½ teaspoon salt
¼ teaspoon nutmeg
1 tablespoon cooking oil
¾ cup flour
1 egg
½ cup milk
¼ teaspoon salt

Mix the beef, pork, pepper, salt and nutmeg together. Form into small patties about 1½" in diameter. Place the oil in a long coffee-cake tin and heat. Put the patties into the tin and brown on both sides. Remove from heat.

Make a batter of the flour, egg, milk and salt. Set aside for about 30 minutes, or until the browned patties are thoroughly cool. Pour the batter over the meat patties, place in a 350° F. oven, and bake for about 30 minutes, or until outer edges of the batter are well browned.

BURGER SAUSAGE ROLLS

½ pound ground chuck
½ pound ground pork
½ teaspoon salt
¼ teaspoon pepper
¼ teaspoon ground cloves
¼ teaspoon garlic powder
1 teaspoon monosodium glutamate
1 egg, separated

Pastry

½ cup vegetable shortening
1 cup all-purpose flour
½ teaspoon salt
3 brimming tablespoons water

Mix the chuck, pork, salt, pepper, cloves, garlic powder
and monosodium glutamate. Add only the egg yolk to the
meat; reserve the white to brush top of pastry. Mix very well
and set aside.

Cut the shortening into the flour with two knives or a
pastry blender. Add the salt and continue to cut until the
mixture is the consistency of bread crumbs. Add the water
and knead the mixture into a dough. Place on a floured board
or pastry cloth and roll into an oval until the dough is about
¼″ thick. Cut into eight pieces about 3″ x 3″.

Form the meat mixture into eight finger-shaped sausages
and sprinkle them lightly with flour on all sides. Place the sausages in the center of each square of pastry. Fold over the two
sides, but leave the ends open. Pinch the pastry tightly so
that the bottoms are well sealed. Make three gashes on the
top of each roll with a sharp knife. Brush the top of each
roll with the egg white, slightly beaten.

Place the rolls on a cookie sheet, leaving about 1″ space
between them. Place in a 400° F. oven for 20 minutes. As
soon as the edges get brown, reduce the heat to 300° F. and
bake for 20 minutes longer. Serve piping hot.

DUTCH SAUSEASONS

The story behind sauseasons (pronounced saw-seasons) is that the Dutch housewives used to make these in the month of November, after the fall butchering. They would bake them and then store them in some safe place outdoors so they could freeze solid. The fishermen would then thaw them as needed, and take them along on the fishing boats to use as a quick snack when the fish were running and the men didn't have time to stop to cook meals.

Filling

1 pound ground lean pork (or half pork and half beef)
1 teaspoon salt
½ teaspoon monosodium glutamate
½ teaspoon ground pepper

Dough

4 cups sifted enriched flour
1 cup lukewarm milk
1½ teaspoons salt
4 tablespoons melted butter or margarine
1 package powdered dry yeast dissolved in ½ cup lukewarm water

Mix the meat, salt, monosodium glutamate and pepper very thoroughly. Set aside in refrigerator while you make the dough.

Place the flour in a large mixing bowl; make a dent in the center and add the milk, salt and melted butter; add the yeast and then stir with a slotted spoon until almost all of the liquid is absorbed. Knead with your hands until the whole ball of dough is shiny and smooth. Form into a large ball and place in a greased mixing bowl to rise. Cover with a cloth and place in the warmest spot in your kitchen. The dough should rise to double its bulk in about 2 hours.

When it has risen, place on a floured board or pastry cloth and knead again for about two minutes. Cut off pieces about the size of an egg, flatten out and place about two tablespoonfuls of the meat mixture, shaped like a little sausage, in the middle. Fold the dough over and around and shape it to look like a miniature loaf of bread about 3″ long. Be sure the dough is sealed all around the meat.

Place the loaves in two rows in a 7″ x 11″ greased coffee-cake tin. When you have used all of the dough, place the pan in a warm place to rise again. When almost doubled in size, place in a 350° F. preheated oven and bake for 1 hour or until the tops are golden brown. During the baking process the little loaves will swell up and fill the whole pan, much in the manner of Parker House rolls. The bottom crust becomes a crisp golden brown, too, as a result of the fat content in the pork.

Sauseasons are equally delicious hot or cold; they make excellent party fare because they can be prepared ahead of time.

BACON BURGER SURPRISE

Batter

2 eggs
¾ cup milk
¾ cup all-purpose flour
1 tablespoon dry yeast, dissolved in ¼ cup lukewarm water
¼ teaspoon salt
1 tablespoon brandy (optional)

Filling

1 pound hamburger
1 egg
¼ cup soft bread crumbs
1 teaspoon minced onion
⅛ teaspoon thyme
⅛ teaspoon nutmeg
½ teaspoon salt
¼ teaspoon pepper
8 to 10 slices bacon
Enough cooking oil for French frying

Beat the eggs until golden yellow. Alternately add the milk and flour and continue beating. Add the dissolved yeast, salt and brandy. Continue to beat for 3 minutes longer. Set aside.

Thoroughly mix the hamburger and the remaining ingredients, with the exception of the bacon and the cooking oil. Place mixture in the refrigerator for 15 minutes, then take out and form into finger-shaped sausages. Wrap each sausage in a slice of bacon, starting at the top and winding barberpole fashion. Place on a piece of waxed paper and return to the refrigerator for 30 minutes.

Dip each chilled sausage wrapped in bacon in the batter and then drop into hot cooking fat until golden brown. Serve piping hot.

HAMBURGER-MACARONI PIE

Pastry

½ cup vegetable shortening
1 cup instant flour
1 teaspoon salt
3 brimming tablespoons water

Filling

1 12-ounce package elbow macaroni
1 pound hamburger
1 small can tomato paste
4 tablespoons Parmesan-Romano cheese
½ teaspoon salt
¼ teaspoon pepper
2 eggs

Cut the shortening into the flour and salt mixture until it is the consistency of bread crumbs. Add the water and continue to cut and blend until you have a stiff dough. Divide into two portions and roll out until you have circles large enough to fill the bottom and top of your favorite pie dish.

Cook the elbow macaroni until tender. Rinse in cold water, drain and set aside. Brown the hamburger until it has separated into lumps about the size of large peas, add the tomato paste, cook for a few seconds longer, then remove from heat. Add the cheese, and stir in the macaroni. Add the salt and pepper and stir again.

Line your pie tin with the pastry. Be sure the outer edges are firmly in place. Pour into the pastry-lined tin the macaroni and meat mixture. Beat the two eggs until they are golden yellow. Pour the eggs over the macaroni-meat mixture. Cover with the remaining pastry, making sure that the edges are well sealed. Pierce with a sharp knife in several places. Place in a preheated 350° F. oven and bake for 35 minutes, or until crust is golden brown. Serve piping hot.

Variations:

Substitute grated American cheese for the Parmesan-Romano.
Substitute grated Swiss cheese for the Parmesan-Romano.
Substitute feta (Greek) cheese for the Parmesan-Romano.
Use half a package of macaroni and add 1 #2 can of niblet-style corn.
Substitute broad noodles for the macaroni.
Substitute rice for the macaroni.
Substitute thin spaghetti for the macaroni

PELMENY, OR MEAT DUMPLINGS

Filling

½ pound lean ground beef
½ pound lean ground pork
½ pound ground veal
1 tablespoon minced onion
½ teaspoon salt
¼ teaspoon pepper
¼ teaspoon nutmeg
⅛ teaspoon marjoram

Dumpling mix

1 cup flour
½ teaspoon salt
½ teaspoon baking powder
1 egg
3 brimming tablespoons cold water

Mix the beef, pork and veal very thoroughly. If you are fortunate enough to have an accommodating butcher, ask him to double grind all of the meat. Add the onion, salt, pepper, nutmeg and marjoram. Mix until the onion and seasonings are thoroughly blended throughout the meat. Set aside while you make the dumplings.

Place the flour in a mixing bowl, stir in the salt and baking powder. Break the egg into the center, add the water and mix thoroughly. Knead into a stiff dough. Now roll the dough out on a floured board until it is about as thin as pie crust. Using a 2″ round cookie cutter, cut circles. Place a teaspoonful of the meat mixture in the center of each circle. Fold up the sides and press the edges together, carefully sealing in all of the meat mixture. You may reroll the portions of the dough left around the circles without fear of its getting tough.

Drop the dumplings into a kettleful of rapidly boiling salted water. When the dumpling rises to the top, remove from the water with a slotted spoon.

Place the cooked dumplings on a heated platter. These dumplings are delicious just as they are; however, if you want to be festive, pour about ¼ cup melted butter or ½ cup sour cream over them. Garnish with parsley if you want to add color.

HAMBURGER PIE CRUST

1 pound ground chuck
½ pound ground pork
1 cup whole wheat flakes, rolled fine
2 eggs, beaten until lemon yellow
1 6-ounce can condensed milk
1 tablespoon grated onion
½ teaspoon garlic juice
1 teaspoon salt
½ teaspoon monosodium glutamate
¼ teaspoon pepper
¼ teaspoon grated nutmeg
1 teaspoon granulated sugar
1 #2 can niblet-style corn, drained
2 canned pimento, cut into ¼" pieces
1 8-ounce can tomato sauce

Mix the chuck and pork together; add the whole wheat flakes, eggs and milk alternately. Stir well; add the onion, garlic juice, salt, monosodium glutamate, pepper, nutmeg and sugar. Mix all very thoroughly. Press the meat mixture over the bottom and sides of a greased pie tin. Mix the corn, pimento and tomato sauce together and pour into the meat-lined tin. Bake in a 350° F. oven, uncovered, for 1 hour. Garnish with chopped parsley if you desire additional color.

Ten other fillings for Hamburger Pie Crust:

1. Substitute 1 #2 can of drained pork and beans for corn and omit the tomato sauce.
2. Substitute 1 8-ounce package of broad egg noodles, boiled until tender, for the corn.
3. Substitute 1 cup of fresh mushrooms and 1 10½-ounce can of cream of mushroom soup for the corn, pimento and tomato sauce.
4. Substitute 1 package frozen lima beans and ½ cup cubed onion for the corn.
5. Substitute 2 cups cooked rice plus 1 10½-ounce can cream of mushroom soup for corn, pimento and tomato sauce.
6. Substitute 1 package frozen green peas and 1 10½-ounce can cream of celery soup for corn, pimento and tomato sauce.
7. Substitute 1 package frozen succotash for the corn.

8. Substitute 1 #2 can beef chow mein for the corn, pimento and tomato sauce. Top with chow mein fried noodles if you like.
9. Substitute 1 #2 can spaghetti in meat sauce for corn, pimento and tomato sauce.
10. Substitute 2 cups boiled macaroni for the corn and sprinkle ¼ cup Parmesan cheese over the top.

TINY HAMBURGERS

1 pound ground round steak
2 tablespoons grated onion
2 egg yolks, beaten until lemon yellow
½ teaspoon salt
3 tablespoons olive oil
⅛ teaspoon salt
2 cups biscuit mix
¾ cup milk
1 tablespoon water
2 egg whites
¼ cup minced parsley

Mix the ground meat, onion, egg yolks and ½ teaspoon salt together. Using a tablespoon, form little patties about the size of silver dollars. Heat the olive oil and fry the patties until they are well browned. Set aside while you make the biscuits.

Mix the ⅛ teaspoon salt into the biscuit mix, add the milk. Stir until the dough forms into a large ball. Place on a lightly floured board and pat flat until it is about ½″ thick. With a small cookie cutter about the size of the meat patties, cut enough biscuits to equal the number of patties. Add the water to the egg whites and beat with a fork. Brush the top of each biscuit with the egg white mixture. Place on a lightly greased cookie tin and bake at 375° F. for 15 minutes, or until they are golden brown.

Sprinkle the minced parsley on top of the meat patties. Cut the biscuits in half and put the meat patties inside. Place in a 350° F. oven for 10 minutes. You can prepare these hamburgers ahead of time and keep them refrigerated until you need them. This is excellent fare for a buffet-style meal.

HAMBURGER MINCEMEAT

2 pounds ground chuck
½ pound suet ground with the chuck
5 tart baking apples, peeled, cored and chopped very fine
1½ cups dark brown sugar
2 cups apple butter
1 tablespoon cider vinegar
¾ cup raisins, chopped fine
¾ cup currants
2 tablespoons bead molasses
1½ teaspoons cinnamon
¼ teaspoon nutmeg
¼ teaspoon cloves
¼ teaspoon allspice
Pinch of mace
1 teaspoon lemon extract
Juice and grated rind of 1 lemon
1 cup water

Cook the meat in a deep saucepan until it loses all of its reddish color and is well done and separated into small pieces. Stir in all of the other ingredients in the order which they are given. Simmer for 1 hour. This mincemeat can be kept for several days in the refrigerator. If you want to use it for holiday cooking, you can preserve it by placing it in a sterilized canning jar with a rubber top closure. This mincemeat can be used in any recipe calling for mincemeat—pie, cookies, scones, cup cakes, etc.

HAMBURGER STUFFED LOAF

1 pound ground chuck
½ pound ground ham
1 cup apple butter
10 slices American cheese, cut into ¼″ cubes
1 small onion, chopped very fine
2 eggs, beaten lemon yellow
1 teaspoon salt
¼ teaspoon pepper
1 loaf white bread, unsliced, Vienna style
3 tablespoons butter

Mix the ground meat with the apple butter, cheese, onion, eggs, salt and pepper. Cut the loaf of bread through the middle, crosswise. Scoop out the soft bread from each half. Shred up the soft bread and add to the meat mixture. Brush the bottom crust of the loaf with the butter and place on a piece of foil large enough to wrap the entire loaf.

Place the meat mixture in the bottom half of the loaf, heaping up a mound to fit the hollow in the top half. Put top half in place and wrap the loaf securely in the foil. Pierce foil in a few places so it can emit the steam.

Place on a baking tin in a 350° F. oven for 1 hour. Fifteen minutes before removing from the oven, open the foil and allow the bread to crisp and brown. Cut loaf in generous slices.

Variations:

Substitute feta (Greek) cheese for American cheese.
Substitute 1½ cups mincemeat for apple butter.
Add 1 cup of chopped raisins.
Add 1 cup of chopped walnuts or pecans.
Substitute 1 cup tart currant jelly for the apple butter.
Substitute Swiss cheese for the American cheese.

SWEDISH MEAT BALLS IN CRUSTS

½ pound ground beef
½ pound ground ham
1 cup instant flour
½ teaspoon salt
1 tablespoon vegetable shortening
⅛ cup milk
½ package dry yeast
2 eggs, beaten

Mix the ham and beef very thoroughly. Form into 20 little meat balls, using the large end of a melon-ball maker. Place the meat balls in a skillet over low heat and let them brown. Shake the pan back and forth so that they will remain round. When all are browned, set aside.

Put the flour in a mixing bowl, mix in the salt and cut in the shortening. Warm the milk just slightly, and stir in the yeast. Pour ⅔ of the beaten egg into the center of the flour, mix slightly and then add the yeast and milk mixture. Knead into a dough. Form dough into 20 little balls and place in a greased cookie tin. Put into a warm place for about 45 minutes, or until the balls have doubled in size. Brush them with the remaining ⅓ of the beaten egg. Place dough balls in a preheated 375° F. oven for 10 minutes. Remove and let cool until you are able to handle them.

With a very sharp knife, cut the bread balls in half. With the tip of a teaspoon remove the soft dough, leaving only the crusty part. In the center place a meat ball, cover with the other half of the bread ball and return the balls to the cookie tin. Place them in a 375° F. oven again, until the outsides are golden brown.

Chapter VI

DEPARTMENT OF
INTERIOR SURPRISES

MOST MEAT PIES call for left-over meat, but the pies in this chapter are all made with fresh hamburger. However, if you happen to have the lean remnants of a beef roast, do not hesitate to add them.

Meat pies could be considered one-dish meals, yet they are too distinctive to be allowed to lose their identity that way.

The pies available in frozen-food packages are usually either chicken, beef or turkey. So a hamburger meat pie can be a pleasant, tasty surprise.

TUCSON MEAT PIE

1½ pounds hamburger
3 tablespoons olive oil
1 large onion, chopped fine
1 large pepper, chopped fine
1 8-ounce can tomato sauce
¼ cup water
1 teaspoon salt
¼ teaspoon pepper
½ teaspoon chili powder
⅛ teaspoon sweet basil
1 teaspoon Accent

Topping

½ cup milk
1 cup Bisquick
2 tablespoons melted butter or margarine

Slowly sauté the hamburger in the olive oil till it is a light, even brown. Add the onion and the green pepper. Pour in the tomato sauce, rinse the can with the water and add this water to the mixture. Add the salt, pepper, chili powder, sweet basil and Accent, and simmer for 15 minutes. Put the entire mixture in a casserole big enough to leave room for the biscuits to rise.

Mix the milk with the Bisquick. On a floured board, knead until smooth and shiny. Roll out the dough until it is about

½" thick. Cut circles, squares or diamond shapes about 2" in diameter. Lay them in a design over the top of the meat mixture. Brush each circle with the melted butter. Place in a 325° F. oven for 30 minutes, or until the biscuits have turned golden brown.

Variations:

Add 1 #2 can niblet-style corn to the hamburger mixture.
Add 1 #2 can black-eyed peas to the hamburger mixture.
Add 1 #2 can butter beans to the hamburger mixture.
Add 1 package frozen lima beans to the hamburger mixture.
Add 1 package frozen carrots and peas to the hamburger mixture.
Add 2 potatoes, cubed in ½" pieces to the hamburger mixture (increase cooking time 10 minutes).
Add 1 #2 can boiled tiny potatoes to the hamburger mixture.

FLANK STEAK STUFFED WITH HAMBURGER

There was a time when flank steak was considered a comparatively cheap cut of meat, but those days are gone. However, the delicious taste of this particular cut is well worth the price. I used to stuff flank steaks with bread until I discovered that when I stuffed them with hamburger they were twice as good.

¾ pound hamburger
1 tablespoon dehydrated parsley
1 tablespoon dehydrated onion
1 cup moist bread crumbs
2 flank steaks, about 1 pound each
1 package dry onion soup mix

Mix the hamburger, parsley, onion, and bread crumbs together very well. Spread the flank steaks out on a cutting board and roll them flatter with your rolling pin.

Put half the hamburger mixture on each steak. Roll up the steaks tightly around the hamburger and fasten with metal skewers. Set out two squares of aluminum foil, each large enough to wrap one steak. Place half of the onion soup mixture and one steak, on each square. Wrap the steaks tightly in the foil and place in a shallow baking pan.

Roast at 375° F. for 1 hour. Slice in generous portions and serve. These steaks are delicious cold, too, and they make excellent sandwiches.

DE LUXE HAMBURGER PIE

2 pounds hamburger
2 tablespoons butter or margarine
1 cup chopped onion
1 can condensed cream of mushroom soup
½ pound cream cheese, at room temperature
½ cup heavy cream
½ teaspoon salt
¼ teaspoon pepper
1 teaspoon Accent
2 tablespoons tomato paste
24 pitted ripe olives, cut into halves
1 package oven-ready biscuits

Brown the hamburger in the butter or margarine, add the onion and continue to cook until the onion begins to get transparent. Meanwhile, with a large blending fork blend the soup, cream cheese and heavy cream. Stir in the salt, pepper, Accent and tomato paste. Add the olives to the meat mixture and then stir the meat mixture into the soup-cream cheese mixture.

Turn all into a greased casserole. Place the biscuits over the top, and put in a preheated 350° F. oven for 30 minutes, or until the biscuits are golden brown.

Variations:

Substitute 1 can cream of celery soup for the mushroom soup.
Substitute 1 can cream of chicken soup for the mushroom soup.
Substitute 1 can chicken gumbo soup for the mushroom soup.
Substitute 1 cup large-curd creamed cottage cheese for the cream cheese.
Substitute 1 cup Swiss cheese for the cream cheese.
Add 1 can niblet-style corn.
Add 1 package frozen lima beans.
Add 1 package frozen carrots and peas.

HAMBURGER PIZZA

1 pound hamburger
½ cup coarsely chopped onion
½ cup coarsely chopped ripe olives
½ cup mushroom stems and pieces
¾ pound mozzarella cheese, diced into ½" pieces
1 small can tomato paste
1 clove garlic, minced
½ teaspoon oregano
¼ teaspoon pepper
½ teaspoon salt
1 14-ounce package refrigerated hot roll mix
2 tablespoons olive oil
¼ cup grated Parmesan cheese

Into a 2-quart mixing bowl put the hamburger, onion, olives, mushrooms and cheese. Add the tomato paste, garlic, oregano, pepper and salt; mix well with a blending fork. At this point, preheat your oven to 450° F.

Divide the hot roll mix into two portions. Knead the biscuit sections together until you have 2 balls of dough about 3" in diameter. Place the balls of dough on a floured board and roll into 2 ⅛"-thick 10"-diameter circles. Place the circles on a floured and buttered cookie sheet. Flute the outer edges of the circles to prevent the pizza mixture from running out. (If it runs out it will stick to the pan.)

Divide the meat mixture in half and spread a half on each of the circles. Brush the olive oil around the fluted edges and over the top. Sprinkle with the cheese. Place in the preheated 450° F. oven and bake from 20 to 25 minutes, or until the edges of the crust are a rich golden brown.

NOGALES TAMALE PIE

4 cups slightly salted boiling water
1 cup yellow corn meal
1 tablespoon olive oil
1 pound hamburger
1 onion, chopped very fine
1 green pepper, chopped very fine
1 #2 can little Italian tomatoes
½ teaspoon salt
½ teaspoon chili powder
Dash Tabasco (optional)
1 package chopped frozen spinach

Put the four cups of boiling water in the top of the double boiler. Fill the bottom with water and turn on the heat. Slowly stir in the corn meal so that no lumps form. Stir until it begins to thicken and coat the spoon. Turn the heat down to simmer and cover the double boiler.

Heat the olive oil in a skillet and add the hamburger to it. Sauté the hamburger until it is golden brown; add the onion and green pepper and sauté for 5 minutes longer. Add the tomatoes, salt, chili powder and Tabasco, if your family likes spicy food. Continue cooking for 10 minutes longer. Then stir in the chopped spinach and remove from the fire.

Grease a 1½-quart casserole. Into the bottom pour half the corn meal mixture, and carefully spoon the meat mixture over it. Top the meat mixture with the remainder of the corn meal. Place in a preheated 350° F. oven for 30 minutes, or until the corn meal topping has turned to golden brown.

Variations:

Substitute 1 package frozen niblet-style corn for the spinach.
Add 1 package frozen lima beans.
Add 1 #2 can butter beans.
Add 1 #2 can lima beans, drained.
Add 1 #2 can red kidney beans.
Add 1 #2 can black-eyed peas.

VEAL BREAST STUFFED WITH HAMBURGER

My family's biggest complaint about economy dishes like stuffed veal breast is that they want more meat. Here is a recipe that has economy and plenty of meat, too.

1 3-pound veal breast
1 teaspoon salt
1 pound hamburger
2 cups moist bread crumbs
1 medium onion, chopped very fine
1 tablespoon paprika

Have your butcher make a pocket in the veal breast. If you purchase meats in a market where they are prepackaged, you can do this yourself with a very sharp paring knife. Just slice a pocket midway between the top and the bottom of the veal breast. It should be large enough to hold the meat and other stuffing ingredients.

Salt the interior of the veal breast. Mix the hamburger with the onions and bread crumbs, and stuff this mixture into the pocket. Fasten the end with skewers. Sprinkle the paprika all over the outside of the veal breast and place in a shallow roasting pan. Cover with foil for the first half of the cooking time. Roast at 350° F. for 1 hour. Then remove foil and bake uncovered for 45 minutes more. The veal should become a rich brown color.

You can make delicious gravy from the pan juices. Remove the meat to a heated platter. Add ½ cup water to the pan juices, and thicken with a heaping tablespoon of flour dissolved in another ¼ cup of water.

EGG-BURGER SURPRISES

1 pound hamburger
½ teaspoon salt
¼ teaspoon pepper
¼ cup instant flour
6 hard-cooked eggs, peeled and cooled
1 raw egg, slightly beaten
1 cup dry bread crumbs or 1 cup crushed shredded wheat
Vegetable oil for deep frying

Mix the hamburger, salt, pepper and flour until smooth. Form into 6 large patties, and place a hard-cooked egg in the center of each. Bring up the sides of each patty and form into a covering all around the egg. Brush with the slightly beaten egg and roll in the bread crumbs or shredded wheat.

Drop into hot fat and fry until the patties turn golden brown. Drain on paper toweling. Cut each patty in half when serving, leaving half of the egg in each section. These can be served hot or cold and create a sensation when used as hors d'oeuvres with cocktails.

HAMBURGER MEAT PUDDING

1 pound hamburger
3 eggs, separated
4 strips bacon, cut into ¼" pieces
¼ cup milk
1 cup soft bread crumbs
1 tablespoon brandy (optional)
¼ teaspoon lemon rind
1 tablespoon parsley, chopped fine
¼ teaspoon pepper
2 tablespoons butter

Place the hamburger in a mixing bowl and add the egg yolks. Add the bacon, milk and bread crumbs. Add the brandy, lemon rind, parsley and pepper. Mix all very well.

Beat the egg whites until they are stiff and dry. Fold them into the meat mixture. Brush a ring mold generously with the butter and carefully spoon in the meat mixture. Try not to pack it too tightly. Place the ring mold in a pan of water and bake in a 350° F. oven for 50 minutes, or until firmly set.

This goes well served with creamed green beans or peas. Mushrooms in cream sauce make it a more elegant dish.

HAMBURGER ONION PIE

Crust

2 cups flour
½ ounce dry yeast
¼ cup lukewarm water
2 eggs
¼ cup milk
1 tablespoon olive oil

Filling

1 pound hamburger
8 medium-sized onions, cut in ¼″ slices
8 strips anchovy
10 black olives, pitted
1 cup canned tomatoes
2 tablespoons olive oil

Place the flour in a mixing bowl; dissolve the yeast in the water and set aside. Break the eggs into the flour, add the milk and olive oil. Stir and, when partially mixed, add the dissolved yeast. Stir and then knead until you have a smooth dough. Set aside to rise for 30 minutes.

Place 1 tablespoonful of olive oil in a skillet; add the hamburger and cook until slightly browned. Add the onions and continue to cook until they are transparent and glazed. Remove from heat and set aside to cool. Cut the anchovy into ¼″ pieces; slice the olives. Reserve half of the olives for the top of the pie. Stir the anchovies, tomatoes and olives into the hamburger mixture.

Put the ball of dough on a floured board and roll out into a circle to fit a large pie tin. Place the dough in the tin, making sure it is well up around the edges. Brush the bottom and sides with the remaining olive oil. Put the hamburger mixture into the pie crust. Decorate the top with the remaining olive slices. Place in a 350° F. oven for 35 minutes, or until the crust is browned. Cut in wedges and serve piping hot.

HAMBURGER DUMPLINGS

6 strips bacon
½ pound hamburger
1 tablespoon dehydrated parsley
1 tablespoon chopped chives, or two scallions, cut very fine
½ teaspoon salt
¼ teaspoon pepper
6 slices white bread soaked in 1 cup milk
3 eggs, beaten until lemon yellow
3 tablespoons butter
¾ cup fine bread crumbs

Dice the bacon very fine and put into a skillet. Fry until it is golden brown and crisp. Remove the bacon from the pan with a slotted spoon and set aside. Now sauté the hamburger in the bacon fat until it is browned. Stir in the parsley, chives, salt and pepper. Remove from heat. Set aside to cool.

Squeeze the milk from the bread and add the bread to the hamburger; now stir in the beaten eggs and mix very well. Form the mixture into small balls about the size of golf balls. Drop into rapidly boiling water and cook for about 12 minutes. Meanwhile, melt the butter and brown the bread crumbs in it. Place the dumplings on a heated platter; sprinkle the browned bread crumbs over the top. Decorate with the tiny pieces of crisp bacon.

PIMENTOS WITH PAPRIKA HAMBURGER

8 fresh pimentos approximately 2-3" in diameter
1 pound hamburger
1 egg
1 tablespoon paprika
1 teaspoon salt
3 tablespoons olive oil

With a very sharp knife, cut around the stem of the pimentos. Scrape out all of the seeds and pulp. Rinse under running water and invert to drain. Mix the hamburger, egg, paprika and salt very thoroughly. Press the meat mixture into the hollow in each of the pimentos. Brush the olive oil over the bottom and sides of a shallow baking tin. Place the pimentos in the tin, cover with aluminum foil and bake in a 350° F. oven for 35 minutes.

This dish goes well with macaroni and cheese or with buttered noodles.

HAMBURGER STUFFING FOR TURKEY OR CHICKEN

2 pounds hamburger
½ cup raisins, chopped very fine
¼ cup chopped onion
¼ cup chopped celery
1 tart apple, chopped very fine
½ pound chestnuts, roasted, peeled and coarsely chopped
½ cup pine nuts
1 cup water
1 cup mincemeat
½ cup instant rice

Brown the hamburger until it is all separated and has lost its reddish color. Add the raisins, onion, celery and apple. Stir in the chestnuts and the pine nuts. Add the water and cook, tightly covered, over a low flame for 1 hour. Stir from time to time, and if it gets too dry add more water. Last, stir in the mincemeat and the rice and simmer for 5 minutes, or until the rice is tender. Let cool until you are able to handle it while stuffing the fowl.

This stuffing can be made the day before and refrigerated until you need it. Never stuff a bird the day before it is to be eaten. Prepare the stuffing separately, and stuff the fowl just before roasting it.

GROUND LAMB TURKEY STUFFING

2 tablespoons butter
½ cup chopped onion
2 pounds ground lean lamb
¼ teaspoon cloves
¼ teaspoon cinnamon
¼ teaspoon nutmeg
1 8-ounce can tomato sauce
1 cup dry bread crumbs
4 tablespoons chopped parsley
½ cup chopped walnuts
1 cup celery, cut into ¼″ pieces
2 eggs, beaten to lemon yellow

Melt the butter in a large saucepan. Add the chopped onion and sauté until transparent. Add the ground lamb and continue to sauté until the lamb is a rich golden brown color. Add the cloves, cinnamon and nutmeg. Add the tomato sauce and simmer over low heat for 30 minutes. Add the bread crumbs, parsley and walnuts. Stir all very well and remove from heat. Let cool. Stir in the celery and then the eggs. Mix all very well. Stuff the turkey, and roast it immediately.

This is enough stuffing for a 12 to 15 pound turkey. For best results, spoon the stuffing in lightly.

HAMBURGER-STUFFED MUSHROOMS

24 very large mushrooms
½ pound very lean hamburger
2 tablespoons melted butter
1 tablespoon dehydrated parsley
1 clove garlic, chopped fine
2 beef bouillon cubes dissolved in ¼ cup hot water
½ teaspoon salt
¼ teaspoon pepper
½ cup soft bread crumbs

Wash the mushrooms in rapidly running water. Drain until they are dry. With a very sharp knife, remove the entire stem from each mushroom. Put these stems in a chopping bowl and chop until the pieces are as small as bread crumbs.

Place the hamburger in a mixing bowl. Add the chopped mushroom stems, 1 tablespoon of the melted butter, the parsley, garlic, bouillon cubes, salt, pepper and bread crumbs. Mix all very well.

Place the mushroom caps, hollow side down, in a baking tin. Brush with the remaining butter and place under the broiler for 10 minutes, or until they begin to get brown. Remove from heat and let them cool until you are able to handle them.

Now fill each hollowed-out mushroom with the meat mixture. Put them back in the baking tin, meat side up. Place in a 400° F. oven for 20 minutes, or until the meat begins to brown. Serve piping hot.

DANISH MEAT PIE

Filling

4 strips of bacon, cut into ¼" pieces
½ pound ground chuck
½ pound lean ground pork
½ pound ground veal
3 tablespoons instant onion flakes
1 clove garlic, chopped fine
¼ teaspoon dill seed
¼ teaspoon celery seed
⅛ teaspoon cloves
½ teaspoon salt
4 twists of pepper mill
1 #2 can apple sauce

Crust

2 cups biscuit mix
¾ cup milk
¼ teaspoon salt

Brown the diced bacon in a skillet. Add the beef, pork and veal and cook until the meat loses its reddish color. Drain off any excess fat. Add the onion flakes and garlic. Stir in the dill seed, celery seed, cloves, salt and pepper. Last, add the apple sauce. Bring to a simmer, cover and continue to simmer for 35 minutes. Remove from heat and set aside to cool.

Mix the biscuit mix with the milk and salt. Knead on a floured board until it is stiff enough to handle. Roll out two 9" circles. Place one circle in a 9" pie tin; flatten it out well, bringing it up over the edge for sealing. Put in the meat filling and top with the other circle of dough. Seal the edges to prevent dripping. Gash the top of the pie in six or seven places so the steam can come out.

Place in a preheated 425° F. oven for 20 minutes. Then reduce the heat to 375° F. and bake for 35 minutes longer, or until crust is golden brown.

Chapter VII
SOUP'S ON

MAKE SOUP FROM HAMBURGER? Impossible, most people would say. Well, I make soup from hamburger, and my family likes it. Hamburger, with its high protein content, is a very logical ingredient for soup. Surely it is more reasonable to make it from hamburger than to make it by boiling soup bones for hours, then cooling, straining, etc. Hamburger takes the labor out of homemade soups. We have instant coffee, instant tea, instant almost everything—why not instant soup?

If you still make soup the old-fashioned way, and like to work hard, there's nothing wrong with that. But if you want delicious quick soups, try the ones in this chapter.

BASIC BROTH FROM HAMBURGER

2 pounds lean hamburger
4 quarts cold water
2 large carrots, diced
1 small onion, diced
1 stalk celery, diced
4 sprigs parsley, minced
½ teaspoon pepper
1 teaspoon salt

Slowly sauté the hamburger in the bottom of a soup kettle. Pour off any fat which may accumulate. Add the water and bring to a boil. Simmer for 1 hour. Skim off any froth which may gather during this time. At the end of the hour, add the vegetables, pepper and salt; cook for another 30 minutes.

This is a delicious light soup to use at the beginning of a hearty meal. It can also be made up, frozen, and later used as the base for other, richer soups.

HAMBURGER FRENCH ONION SOUP

1 tablespoon butter
½ pound hamburger
10 medium-sized onions, sliced very thin
1 can beef consommé or stock
1 cup water
2 beef bouillon cubes

Brown the butter in the bottom of your soup kettle. Add the hamburger and fry until very brown and well separated. Add the sliced onions, consommé, water and bouillon cubes and simmer for 30 minutes.

Serve with squares of buttered toast topped with Parmesan cheese.

HAMBURGER MINESTRONE

1 pound hamburger
2 tablespoons olive oil
2 medium-sized onions, sliced thin
⅛ teaspoon sweet marjoram
1 clove garlic
½ bay leaf
2 #2 cans red kidney beans
1 #2 can tomatoes
2 cups shredded white cabbage
1 cup cooked rice
1 cup water (optional)
1 teaspoon salt
¼ teaspoon pepper
½ teaspoon Accent

Sauté the hamburger in the olive oil until it is broken up. Add the onions, marjoram, garlic and bay leaf and sauté for 5 minutes longer. Mash the kidney beans in their own liquid with a potato masher, or put them through your food blender. Add the beans to the meat mixture, along with the tomatoes. Continue to cook over a very low flame for 45 minutes. Keep tightly covered during this period.

Ten minutes before serving time, add the shredded cabbage and the rice. Simmer for 10 minutes. At this point if you feel that this soup is too thick for your family, add the optional cup of water and simmer for a few minutes longer. Add the salt, pepper and Accent. Let stand for a few seconds and then serve.

This soup is excellent if garnished with a heaping teaspoonful of grated Parmesan cheese on each bowl. A very thin slice of lemon floated on top of the soup is also an excellent garnish.

HAMBURGER CHOWDER

1 pound hamburger
1 tablespoon butter
3 large onions, sliced thin
4 stalks celery, cut into ¼" pieces
3 cups water
4 medium raw potatoes, cut into ½" cubes
1 teaspoon salt
4 peppercorns
1 teaspoon Accent
2 packages frozen mixed garden vegetables

Use a 1½ quart or larger saucepan for this soup. Slowly sauté the hamburger in the butter until it is a rich dark brown in color. Add the onions and celery and cook until the onions are slightly glazed.

Add the water and the diced potatoes and cook until the edges of the potatoes are slightly transparent. Now add the salt, peppercorns and Accent. Simmer for 5 minutes.

Add the two packages of frozen vegetables and cook *uncovered* for ten minutes, or until the green beans in the vegetable mixture are easily pierced with a fork.

It is very important that you leave off the cover for the last ten minutes of cooking; this insures that your soup will have that magazine-picture look when you serve it. Covering changes the color of fresh vegetables from bright to drab.

Served with saltines, this is a meal in itself.

Variations:

Add 2 fresh tomatoes, cubed in ¼" pieces.
Add 1 #2 can tomatoes.
Add ½ package chopped spinach.
Substitute 1 package frozen peas and carrots for the mixed vegetables.
Substitute 2 packages frozen baby limas for the mixed vegetables.

HAMBURGER-RED BEAN SOUP

1 pound hamburger
3 tablespoons butter or margarine
2 #2 cans red kidney beans
2 medium-sized onions, sliced very thin
2 medium-sized potatoes, washed but not peeled, cut into
   ½" cubes
4 cups water
1 teaspoon monosodium glutamate
1 teaspoon salt
¼ teaspoon pepper
1 cup heavy cream
1 egg, beaten to a lemon yellow

Sauté the hamburger in the butter or margarine until slightly browned and fairly well separated. Add the kidney beans just as they come from the cans, liquid and all. Add the onions and potatoes. Add the water, and bring to a boil for 10 minutes. Add the monosodium glutamate, salt and pepper. Remove soup from the stove and let cool for a few minutes.

Combine the cream and egg, and add about a half cup of the broth from the soup. Stir well; then add this mixture to the soup, stirring constantly while doing so. Return to heat for 5 minutes.

Serve piping hot. Garnish with grated Parmesan-Romano cheese, if desired.

HAMBURGER CAULIFLOWER SOUP

1 small head cauliflower or 1 package frozen cauliflower
3 tablespoons butter
1 pound hamburger
¼ cup chopped onion
1 small tomato, diced
8 cups hot water
1 teaspoon salt
¼ teaspoon pepper
1 teaspoon Accent
1 cup elbow macaroni

Thoroughly wash the cauliflower under rapidly running water. Break into blossom pieces, and stand aside in a dish of salted water. (If you use frozen cauliflower, this is not necessary.)

Heat the butter in the bottom of a soup kettle and add the hamburger. Brown the hamburger slightly and then add the onion and the diced tomato. Drain the cauliflower and add to the meat mixture, along with two cups of hot water. Cover tightly and simmer for 30 minutes, then add the salt, pepper and Accent. Now add the remainder of the water and the dry macaroni.

Cook until the macaroni is tender. Serve with a sprinkle of Parmesan cheese over each bowl.

RICHER HAMBURGER CAULIFLOWER SOUP

1 pound hamburger
3 tablespoons butter
8 cups water
1 large head cauliflower or 3 packages frozen cauliflower
3 tablespoons cornstarch
3 cups milk
¼ cup grated Parmesan-Romano cheese
1 teaspoon salt
¼ teaspoon pepper
½ teaspoon Accent
2 egg yolks

Sauté the hamburger in the butter until slightly browned. Add the water and bring to a rolling boil. Meanwhile, clean the fresh cauliflower under running water. Break up into flowers and, with your salad chopping knife, chop very fine. Add the chopped cauliflower to the hamburger broth. Turn flame down to simmer.

Meanwhile, put water in the bottom of the double boiler and bring to a boil. Stir the cornstarch into the milk until all is dissolved. Put the milk and cornstarch in the top of the double boiler and cook until the mixture begins to coat the spoon. Stir constantly during this time. As soon as it has thickened, add the cheese. Turn the flame down low enough just to keep the mixture warm.

Add the salt, pepper and Accent to the hamburger-cauliflower mixture. Now take ½ cup of this mixture and stir it into the thickened milk mixture. This is to prevent curdling when you add the milk mixture to the soup.

Add all of the milk mixture to the hamburger-cauliflower broth. Remove from the stove and, after it has cooled for a few minutes, stir in the beaten egg yolks. Serve immediately. Garnish with grated Parmesan cheese if desired.

HAMBURGER BEAN SOUP

1 pound hamburger
1 tablespoon butter or margarine
¼ teaspoon rosemary
¼ cup chopped parsley
3 cloves garlic, minced
1 tablespoon flour
1 small tomato, diced, or ¼ cup tomato sauce
½ teaspoon salt
¼ teaspoon pepper
1 teaspoon Accent
8 cups water
1 cup navy or northern beans, soaked overnight

Sauté the hamburger in the butter or margarine until slightly browned. Add the rosemary, parsley and garlic and sauté five minutes longer. Sprinkle the flour over the sautéed meat and herbs, stirring well. Add the diced tomato, salt, pepper and Accent. Slowly add the water. Bring to a rolling boil and turn the heat down to simmer.

Now add the drained beans and simmer for two hours. If the soup is too thick, add a little more water. The beans should break easily against the side of the kettle when the soup is done.

Serve with croutons.

Variations:

Add 1 package frozen mixed vegetables
Add 1 package baby lima beans

HAMBURGER-POTATO SOUP

4 slices lean bacon, cut into ¼" pieces
1 pound hamburger
3 cups boiling water
½ teaspoon salt
¼ teaspoon pepper
1 teaspoon monosodium glutamate
2 medium-sized onions, sliced very thin
8 medium-sized potatoes, washed but not peeled, diced in ½" squares
1 tablespoon cornstarch
2 cups milk
2 sprigs of parsley, minced, or 1 tablespoon dehydrated parsley

Put the small pieces of bacon into the bottom of a soup kettle; place over a low flame and sauté until the bacon is golden brown. Drain off any excess fat. Add the hamburger and cook and stir until it is all uniformly broken into small pieces and is just beginning to get brown.

Add the water, salt, pepper and monosodium glutamate. When all comes to a rapid boil, add the onions and potatoes. Turn the heat down to simmer and cook slowly for 30 minutes. Do not overcook the potatoes, for half the joy of potato soup is being able to bite into a piece of potato with its own good flavor. Remove from the heat when the edges of the potatoes begin to look slightly transparent.

Stir the cornstarch into the milk, making sure all is dissolved. Slowly, stirring all the while, add the cornstarch-milk mixture to the soup. Cook for 5 minutes longer. Just before serving, stir in the parsley.

Variations:

Add 1 package frozen mixed vegetables.
Add 1 package frozen baby lima beans.
Add 1 package frozen cream-style corn.
Add 1 package frozen peas and carrots.

HAMBURGER-SPINACH SOUP

1 pound lean ground chuck
1 tablespoon butter
2 packages chopped frozen spinach
2 cups milk or half milk and half cream, if you like it rich
½ teaspoon salt
4 twists of pepper mill
¼ teaspoon nutmeg
2 tablespoons cornstarch
¼ cup water

Brown the chuck in the butter. Add the frozen spinach and cook till thoroughly defrosted. Do not cover. Stir in the milk, add the salt, pepper and nutmeg. Simmer for 5 minutes. Thoroughly mix the cornstarch and water. Very slowly, add to the spinach-meat mixture. Stir until thickened. Serve with a dash of nutmeg over each bowl, if desired.

SPINACH SOUP WITH HAMBURGER

1 tablespoon butter
1 pound hamburger
1 cup water
1 package frozen shredded spinach
4 tablespoons cornstarch
1 quart milk
½ teaspoon salt
¼ teaspoon pepper
1 teaspoon monosodium glutamate

Place the butter in the bottom of a soup kettle and melt slowly. Add the hamburger and sauté until it is browned and broken up. Add the water, along with the frozen spinach, and simmer, uncovered, until the spinach is thawed and tender.

Stir the cornstarch into the milk and place over a very low flame. Stir constantly until the mixture begins to thicken. Add several spoonfuls of the meat-spinach mixture to the cornstarch and milk. Then turn the entire milk mixture into the meat-spinach mixture. Now add the salt, pepper and monosodium glutamate; cook for 5 minutes longer, uncovered, over a low flame.

Serve piping hot, with croutons.

HAMBURGER-FRENCH PEA SOUP

1 tablespoon butter
1 medium onion, cut in ⅛" slices
1 pound ground chuck
1 #2 can baby green peas, not drained
1 small head lettuce, shredded very fine
1 medium-sized leek, cut sliver thin
3 tablespoons parsley, chopped very fine
1 teaspoon sugar
½ teaspoon salt
¼ teaspoon pepper
2 cups beef stock or 2 cups water with 4 bouillon cubes dissolved in it
2 cups half and half cream

Melt the butter in a skillet and cook the onion until it is glazed. Add the meat and cook until it loses its reddish color. Set aside.

In a soup kettle place the green peas, liquid and all; add the lettuce, leek, parsley, sugar, salt and pepper. Add the meat stock and bring to a rolling boil; cook, uncovered, for

10 minutes, or until the vegetables can be mashed with a fork.

Strain the vegetable mixture through a fine sieve. Work the vegetables through the sieve until they are reduced to a smooth paste. Return to the soup kettle and add the hamburger. Bring to a simmer for 5 minutes. Now take a half cup of the mixture and stir it into the cream; then add the cream to the vegetables and simmer for 5 minutes longer. This is to prevent curdling and to give the soup a creamy consistency.

Serve with toasted croutons.

GREEK LAMB SOUP

2 tablespoons butter or margarine
1 pound ground lean lamb
4 cups water
½ teaspoon salt
¼ teaspoon pepper
1 bay leaf
1 tablespoon dehydrated parsley
1 leek, sliced fine
1 large carrot, peeled and diced
3 stalks of celery, diced
1 small celery root, diced
1 large parsnip, peeled and diced
3 tablespoons instant flour
1 cup frozen peas

Melt the butter or margarine in a skillet and brown the lamb until it is all broken apart. Place the water in a kettle along with the salt, pepper, bay leaf and parsley. Bring to a rolling boil. Strain the browned lamb, saving the fat. Place the strained lamb in the boiling water. Turn the heat down to simmer.

Return the lamb drippings to the skillet and brown the leek, carrot, celery, celery root and parsnip. Sprinkle the flour over the vegetables and stir and turn until the flour is browned too.

Take 1 cup of the simmering meat broth and pour it over the vegetables. Continue to cook until the parsnip cubes are tender; then add the vegetables to the meat broth. Stir in the frozen peas and cook for 5 minutes longer.

Serve with rounds of toast topped with Parmesan cheese.

HUNGARIAN MEAT BALL SOUP

4 strips of bacon cut into ¼" squares
1 large onion, sliced
1 pound hamburger
½ teaspoon salt
4 twists of pepper mill
2 teaspoons paprika
⅛ teaspoon thyme
⅛ teaspoon marjoram
1 clove garlic, minced
4 cups stock
2 tablespoons flour
¼ cup water
3 cooked potatoes, diced in ½" pieces

Place the diced bacon in the bottom of the soup kettle and fry until it is a crisp golden brown. Add the onion to the bacon and its drippings. Sauté it until it is transparent and just turning brown.

Form the hamburger into tiny meat balls about ¾" in diameter. As you form them, add them to the onion-bacon mixture. Shake the pan back and forth between additions so that the meat balls brown on all sides; add the salt, pepper, paprika, thyme, marjoram and garlic. Add one cup of the stock, and let simmer for about 20 minutes. Mix the flour in the water, being careful that there are no lumps. Slowly add this to the meat mixture. Bring to a simmer again. Gradually add the rest of the soup stock and simmer for 20 minutes longer. Put in the diced potatoes just before serving.

HAMBURGER, POTATO AND LEEK SOUP

2 tablespoons butter
1 pound ground chuck
6 to 8 leeks, white part only, sliced in ⅛" pieces
½ cup celery, chopped fine
3 cups sliced raw potatoes
3 cups meat stock, or 3 cups water with 3 bouillon cubes
    dissolved in it
½ teaspoon salt
5 whole black peppercorns
2 cups half and half cream
1 tablespoon chopped parsley
1 tablespoon chopped chives

Melt the butter in a large saucepan. Add the chuck and cook until it loses its reddish color. Add the leeks, celery, potatoes and stock. Add the salt and peppercorns. Cover and simmer until the potatoes can be mashed with a fork against the side of the kettle. Add about a half cup of the soup broth to the cream. Mix well, then add to the soup. Stir while you are adding the cream. Simmer for an additional 10 minutes.

Serve in a large soup tureen garnished with chopped parsley and chives. Serve piping hot, with saltines.

LAMB SOUP

1 pound ground lean lamb
3 tablespoons butter
1 package frozen chopped spinach
6 green onions (shallots)
½ teaspoon paprika
1 quart water
½ cup precooked rice
8 peppercorns
3 egg yolks
½ cup sour cream

Brown the lamb in the butter until it is separated and about the size of large peas. Add the spinach. Slice the shallots into ¼" pieces; do not use too much of the green portion, as this will make the flavor very harsh. Add the shallots to the spinach and the lamb. Add the paprika and water and then stir in the rice. Add the peppercorns. Cook for about 14 minutes longer, or until the rice is tender.

Beat the egg yolks until they are golden yellow; add the sour cream to the eggs and beat again. Remove the soup from the heat and let cool for a few minutes. Take about a half cup of the soup stock and add to the cream and egg mixture. Stir well; then add the cream and egg mixture to the soup. Return to the heat for 5 minutes more. Stir continuously during this time. Serve with croutons.

BELGIAN HAMBURGER SOUP

4 potatoes, scrubbed very clean
1 cup celery, chopped
1 small can tomato paste
¾ cup chopped onion
2 cloves garlic, cut in small pieces
⅛ teaspoon thyme
½ teaspoon salt
4 twists of pepper mill
1½ quarts water
1 pound hamburger

Chop the whole potatoes (unpeeled) very fine. Place potatoes, celery, tomato paste, onion, garlic, thyme, salt and pepper in the water. Bring to a rapid boil, and then turn heat down to simmer. Simmer for about 1½ hours, stirring occasionally. Brown the hamburger over moderate heat. When it is all separated and about the size of peas, remove from heat and drain off all accumulated fat.

Place the vegetable mixture in a large colander or a Foley food mill. Save the liquid in a separate bowl. Force the vegetables through the colander. Add the hamburger and the puréed vegetables to the stock. Reheat all together and serve.

HAMBURGER-PEA SOUP

2 cups dried whole peas
1 pound hamburger
¼ cup chopped onion
2 tablespoons butter or margarine
1 tablespoon dehydrated parsley flakes
½ teaspoon salt
¼ teaspoon ground pepper or 4 twists of pepper mill
¼ cup cream or condensed milk
6-8 pieces of rosemary

Soak the peas overnight in water; drain and cover again with cold water. Bring to a rolling boil and then turn heat down to simmer until the peas are tender. Brown the hamburger in the butter or margarine, add the onion, parsley flakes, salt and pepper and continue to cook until the onion is glazed and transparent.

Add the hamburger mixture to the peas, stir in the cream and add the rosemary. Simmer for 10 minutes longer. Serve with toasted croutons.

CHILI

1 pound hamburger
2 tablespoons butter or margarine
½ cup celery, chopped fine
½ cup onion, chopped fine
1 teaspoon salt
4 twists of pepper mill
1 teaspoon chili powder
2 #2 cans of tomatoes
1 cup water
1 8-ounce package elbow macaroni

Brown the hamburger in the butter or margarine. Add the celery and onion and cook until tender. Add the salt, pepper and chili powder. Stir in the tomatoes and water. Add the elbow macaroni as it comes from the package. Simmer for 1 hour, or until the macaroni is tender. Serve piping hot with saltines.

CHILI CON CARNE

1 tablespoon butter or margarine
2 large onions, diced in ¼" pieces
1 pound ground chuck
1 teaspoon salt
1 teaspoon chili powder
1 cup diced raw potatoes
1 small green pepper, diced in ¼" pieces
½ cup chopped celery
1 #2 can tomatoes
1 10½-ounce can condensed tomato soup
2 #2 cans kidney beans (do not drain)

Melt the butter or margarine in the bottom of a large saucepan. Add the onions and cook until they are tender and transparent. Add the chopped meat and continue to cook until the meat loses its reddish color. Add the salt and chili powder. Continue to cook for a few seconds longer.

Add the potatoes, green pepper, celery, tomatoes and tomato soup. Simmer for 15 minutes longer, or until the edges of the potato cubes become transparent. Last, add the kidney beans and simmer for 15 minutes longer. If the chili is too thick for your taste, add a little tomato juice.

Serve with crisp crackers.

Chapter VIII

QUICKIES

QUICKIE CUTLETS

½ pound ground chuck
½ pound ground veal
½ teaspoon salt
4 twists of pepper mill
4 slices American process cheese
2 eggs, well beaten
1 cup dry bread crumbs
Vegetable oil for deep frying

Mix the chuck, veal, salt and pepper very well. Form into 8 patties. Fold the pieces of cheese in four, place on one of the patties, then cover with another patty. Press the edges together so the cheese is well sealed inside.

Brush each side of the patty with the beaten egg and then dip into the bread crumbs. If necessary, press the bread crumbs into the surface. Drop into deep oil and fry until they are golden brown. Serve with hashed brown potatoes and creamed green beans.

HAMBURGER BREAKFAST SURPRISE

The hue and cry for high-protein breakfasts can be met with this delicious dish.

1 pound ground chuck
½ pound lean ground pork
1 tablespoon dehydrated parsley
½ teaspoon salt
½ teaspoon pepper
1 cup white bread, soaked in milk to cover
1 cup dry bread crumbs, rolled fine
3 tablespoons butter
6 eggs

Mix the chuck, pork, parsley, salt and pepper very well. Squeeze the milk out of the bread and add the bread to the meat mixture. Discard what little milk is left. Mix all well, and form into 6 4″ diameter patties. Dip each patty into the fine bread crumbs.

Melt the butter in a skillet with a tight-fitting cover. Sauté the patties on one side until golden brown. Turn the patties over and, with the back of a tablespoon, make an indentation large enough to hold an egg. Carefully break an egg into each hollow. Cover the pan and cook for 5 minutes, or until the eggs are completely set and firm.

TOMATOES WITH FILLING

8 3″ diameter tomatoes
1 pound hamburger
1 cup instant rice
½ teaspoon salt
4 twists of pepper mill
1 onion, minced
⅛ teaspoon thyme
⅛ teaspoon marjoram
⅛ teaspoon oregano
1 tablespoon olive oil

With a very sharp knife, cut away the stem portion and scoop out the inside of each tomato. Place the pulp in a bowl, and add to it the hamburger, the rice just as it comes from the package, the salt, pepper, onion and herbs.

Mix all very well. Stuff each of the tomato shells with the meat mixture and place in an oiled flat baking dish or in individual casseroles. Bake for 35 minutes in a 350° F. oven.

It is wise to allow two stuffed tomatoes per person, as this dish is very tasty and one apiece will not be enough.

QUICK MEAT PIE

1 pound hamburger
1 can deviled ham (4-ounce size)
1 8-ounce package cream cheese, at room temperature
1 can chicken gumbo soup
1 package frozen corn
1 onion, minced
10 ripe olives, pitted and sliced
1 can oven-ready biscuits

Brown the hamburger in a skillet. Remove from heat and stir in the deviled ham, cheese and soup. Break up the frozen corn so that the kernels are separated, and add to the meat mixture. Stir in the onion and the olives. Place all in a deep casserole and top with the biscuits.

Bake at 375° F. for 30 minutes, or until the biscuits are golden brown. Serve with a parsley garnish, if you like.

SAGE AND RICE HAMBURGER

1 pound hamburger
1 egg, slightly beaten
½ cup soft bread crumbs
4 tablespoons butter
1 medium-sized onion, cut into ¼" pieces
1 clove garlic, sliced very thin
2 cups warm water with 3 beef bouillon cubes dissolved in it
2 cups precooked rice
½ teaspoon powdered sage
½ cup Parmesan-Romano cheese

Mix the hamburger with the slightly beaten egg and the bread crumbs. Form into 8 small patties about 2" in diameter. Melt the butter in a large skillet with a tight-fitting cover. Brown the meat patties on both sides in the butter. Remove the patties with a spatula and set in a warm place. Reserve the remaining butter.

Sauté the onion and garlic in the remaining butter until the onion is slightly transparent. Add the bouillon to the onion. Add the rice just as it comes from the package; then add the sage. Stir very well. Cook over low heat, tightly covered, for 10 minutes, or until all of the rice has doubled in size and is tender and separated.

Place the sage rice on a heated platter with the hamburger patties around the edge. Sprinkle the rice with the cheese. Place under the broiler for 3 or 4 minutes, or until the cheese begins to brown. Serve piping hot.

GREEN RICE WITH HAMBURGER

2 tablespoons butter
1 pound hamburger
1 onion, chopped fine
2 cups water
2 cups instant rice
½ teaspoon salt
1 can strained baby food spinach
2 tablespoons parsley, chopped fine

Melt the butter in a skillet and brown the hamburger. Add the onion and continue to cook until it is transparent.

Place the water in a saucepan and bring to a rapid boil. Stir in the rice and add the salt. Cover tightly and cook for 5 minutes, or until all the kernels are separated. Then stir in the strained spinach. Add the hamburger and onion. Place on a heated platter and garnish with the parsley.

QUICK MEAT SAUCE OVER RICE

1 pound hamburger
2 tablespoons cornstarch
2 cups V-8 vegetable juice cocktail
1 beef bouillon cube
½ teaspoon salt
2 cups precooked rice
2 cups water

Brown the hamburger in a skillet until it loses its reddish color. Stir the cornstarch into the V-8 juice and pour over the hamburger. Add the bouillon cube and salt. Cook for 8 minutes, or until thickened.

Put the rice in a saucepan with the water and cook until all the liquid has been absorbed and the rice is tender. Place the rice in a large serving bowl, make a hollow in the center and pour in the thickened meat sauce.

Ten Variations for the Meat Sauce:

1. Stir in #2 can drained niblet-style corn 5 minutes before serving.
2. Substitute 1 8-ounce package broad cooked noodles for the rice.
3. Add 2 packages frozen lima beans 5 minutes before serving.
4. Add 2 packages frozen peas with little onions 5 minutes before serving.
5. Omit the rice and stir into the meat sauce 1 #2½ can pork and beans.
6. Add 2 packages frozen zucchini squash 5 minutes before serving.
7. Add 2 packages frozen green beans 5 minutes before serving.
8. Add 1 #2 can mushroom stems and pieces, drained, 5 minutes before serving.
9. Add #2 can yellow butter beans 5 minutes before serving.
10. Omit the rice and add 2 #2 cans macaroni and cheese 5 minutes before serving.

HAMBURGER NESTS

1 pound ground chuck
½ teaspoon salt
¼ teaspoon pepper
1 tablespoon minced onion
1 tablespoon olive oil
2 tablespoons dehydrated parsley
8 eggs
1 cup heavy cream sauce
4 tablespoons Parmesan cheese

Mix the chuck very thoroughly with the salt, pepper and minced onion. Grease 4 individual casserole dishes with the olive oil. After dipping your fingers in ice water, divide the meat into 4 equal portions. Line the sides and bottoms of the casseroles with the meat. Place the casseroles on a cookie sheet under the broiler for 5 minutes, or until the tops begin to brown. Then remove from the oven. Turn oven from broil down to 350° F. and close door to keep hot.

Very carefully, break 2 eggs into each of the casseroles; sprinkle with dehydrated parsley. Return casseroles to the oven (still at 350° F.) for 8 minutes, or until egg whites have set firmly. Remove from oven, but leave heat at 350° F.

Place 3 tablespoonfuls of the cream sauce on each of the casseroles, then sprinkle with cheese. Return to oven for 5 minutes longer. Serve piping hot with wedges of toast and a tossed green salad. If you have oven-to-table dishes you can serve direct from the casseroles; otherwise, invert onto plates.

Chapter IX
MEAT BALLS GALORE

MEAT BALLS made out of ground meat is a universal dish; you can find variations of it wherever there are people. India has its meat ball dishes, Japan offers its contributions and the European countries have given us innumerable variations. In this chapter we hope you find a few new ones to add to your list of meat ball favorites. A whole book could be written on meat balls alone, so I am giving you only the most unique ones I know.

A friend has passed on to me a trick for successful meat ball cookery that you might like to try. After the meat balls have been formed, plunging them momentarily into rapidly boiling water keeps them from losing their round shape during the remainder of the cooking time. The boiling water does not change the taste; indeed, it actually seals in the flavor of the meat.

If you like to make small meat balls about the size of walnuts, there is one kitchen gadget which is a timesaver—the melon-ball maker. This is a ladlelike gadget with two sizes of round scoops, small on one end and large on the other. This type of melon-ball maker can be found in almost any housewares department or variety store. Invest in one; you will find it indispensable. For larger meat balls, you will find an ice cream scoop a boon.

So here are my most unusual meat ball recipes. I have a lot more favorites, but you probably already have many of the more common ones in your own recipe file.

SWEET AND SOUR MEAT BALLS WITH RICE

1 pound ground beef
½ pound ground lean pork
2 eggs
1 teaspoon Accent
½ teaspoon salt
4 twists of pepper mill
3 onions, sliced very thin
1 cup celery, sliced very thin
½ cup water
¼ cup lemon juice (or you may substitute vinegar if you
like)
¼ cup light brown sugar
1 teaspoon bead molasses
1 tablespoon soy sauce
2 cups instant rice
2 cups water
2 tablespoons chopped almonds (optional)
1 tablespoon chopped pimento (optional)

Mix the beef, pork, eggs, Accent, salt and pepper very thoroughly. Form into meat balls about the size of walnuts. Plunge the meat balls into very rapidly boiling water, one at a time; remove them to drain as soon as they are firm. This will help them stay nice and round during the remainder of the cooking time. Brown the meat balls in a large frying pan. Instead of turning with a spatula, move the pan back and forth so that they roll while frying and browning. After they are all a golden brown, add the onions and celery. Continue to cook until the onions are transparent and the celery is tender.

Mix the water, lemon juice, sugar, molasses and soy sauce and pour over the meat balls. Bring to a boil, then turn the heat down to simmer for 20 minutes.

Cook the rice in the water in an uncovered pan for 3 to 5 minutes. Cover tightly and set aside for 5 minutes. Serve mounds of fluffy rice with the meat ball mixture poured over it. Garnish with almonds and pimento for a gourmet touch, if desired.

MEAT BALLS IN RED WINE

2 pounds ground chuck
1 egg, slightly beaten
3 tablespoons flour
½ teaspoon paprika
3 tablespoons butter
3 cups red wine (Burgundy or claret)
1 clove garlic, sliced
¼ cup warm water with 2 bouillon cubes dissolved in it
1 bay leaf
¼ teaspoon thyme
1 stalk celery, cut very fine
1 #2 can small onions
1 #2 can mushroom stems and pieces
1 8-ounce package wide noodles
3 quarts rapidly boiling slightly salted water
1 tablespoon butter or margarine

Mix the ground meat with the egg. Form into meat balls about the size of golf balls. Mix the flour and paprika and roll the meat balls in the mixture. Melt the 3 tablespoons of butter in a skillet and brown the meat balls on all sides. Remove them from the skillet, saving the drippings. Place the meat balls in a 1½-quart casserole. Over them, pour the red wine; add the garlic, bouillon, bay leaf, thyme and celery. Cover and place in a 350° F. oven for 45 minutes.

Reheat the drippings in the skillet and add the drained onions and mushrooms. Sauté until they are slightly browned. Add to the meat ball mixture and continue to braise at 350° F. for 15 minutes longer.

Boil the noodles in the 3 quarts of water. Drain, and add the butter or margarine. Place the noodles on a large heated serving platter; cover with the meat balls. Serve at once. This is enough for 8 servings.

MEAT BALLS WITH SAUERBRATEN GRAVY

2 pounds hamburger
1 egg
1 teaspoon salt
¼ teaspoon pepper
¼ cup onion, chopped fine
1 tablespoon dehydrated parsley
1 cup soft bread crumbs
¼ cup flour
2 tablespoons butter or margarine
1 cup meat stock, or 2 bouillon cubes dissolved in 1 cup water
¼ cup water
2 tablespoons cider vinegar
2 tablespoons sugar
¼ teaspoon nutmeg
⅛ teaspoon ground cloves
1 bay leaf
3-4 2″ diameter ginger snaps

Mix the hamburger with the egg, salt, pepper, onion and parsley. Add the bread crumbs. Mix and knead very well. Form into meat balls about the size of golf balls. Plunge into boiling water momentarily to seal in the flavor and help the meat balls retain their shape. Then roll them in the flour. (This acts as a browning agent.)

Melt the butter in a large skillet and brown the meat balls in it. When they are golden brown, add the stock and simmer for 5 minutes. Mix the water, vinegar, sugar, nutmeg and cloves and add to the meat. Break up the bay leaf into 3 or 4 pieces and add. Let simmer for 10 minutes longer. Crush the ginger snaps and add. Turn each meat ball over so that it is thoroughly coated with gravy. If you would like a more sour gravy, add another tablespoonful of cider vinegar. Simmer for an additional 10 minutes. Should the gravy get too thick, add more water.

Serve on a heated platter over buttered noodles or dumplings.

MEAT BALLS IN CARAWAY

2 potatoes, scrubbed but not peeled
1 medium-sized onion
1 pound ground chuck
1 teaspoon seasoned salt
4 twists of pepper mill
2 eggs, beaten to a lemon yellow
1 tablespoon dehydrated parsley
3 tablespoons flour
1 teaspoon paprika
3 cups water
3 beef bouillon cubes
½ teaspoon caraway seeds
½ teaspoon grated lemon peel

Cut the potato into chunks and put it into your food blender. When it is chopped very fine, add the onion and continue to blend for a few seconds longer. Add the blended potato and onion to the ground meat, along with the salt, pepper, eggs and parsley. Mix all very well and form into meat balls about the size of golf balls. Mix the flour and paprika thoroughly and roll the meat balls in it. Make sure they are thoroughly coated with flour.

Bring the water to a rolling boil and carefully drop in the meat balls. Add the bouillon cubes and turn the heat down to simmer. Cover tightly and simmer for 35 minutes.

At the end of this time, stir in the caraway seeds and the lemon peel. Continue to simmer for 10 minutes longer. If the gravy is not thick enough, leave the cover off during this last ten minutes.

This dish goes well with noodles, rice or plain boiled potatoes.

SERBIAN MEAT BALLS

½ pound ground lamb
½ pound ground beef
½ teaspoon salt
¼ teaspoon pepper
1 tablespoon olive oil
3 eggs, separated
1 teaspoon yoghurt
Dash of salt
Dash of pepper
1 teaspoon paprika

Mix the lamb and beef together thoroughly. Season with the ½ teaspoon salt and ¼ teaspoon pepper and form into meat balls about the size of golf balls. Heat the olive oil in a deep skillet and brown the meat balls on all sides.

Meanwhile, beat the egg yolks until they are light and lemon colored. Stir the yoghurt into the egg yolks, mixing very well. Add a dash of salt, a dash of pepper, and the paprika. Mix again. Beat the egg whites until they stand in peaks. Fold into the yoghurt-egg yolk mixture.

Remove the meat balls from the skillet and place them in a deep baking dish. Pour over this the yoghurt-egg mixture. Cook at 350° F. for about 20 minutes, or until the sauce is thickened.

Serve with mashed or plain boiled potatoes.

MEAT BALLS IN MUSTARD SAUCE

1 pound hamburger
2 tablespoons flour
1 teaspoon salt
4 twists of pepper mill
1 teaspoon Accent
1 tablespoon butter or margarine
3 cups meat stock
2 tablespoons dry mustard
1 tablespoon brown sugar
½ teaspoon cocoa

Mix the hamburger with the flour, salt and pepper. Add the Accent and mix thoroughly. Melt the butter or margarine in a deep skillet. Form the ground meat into meat balls about the size of golf balls. Place in the skillet and cook until they are golden brown.

Add the meat stock and simmer for 10 minutes. Then remove approximately ¾ cup of the broth and stir the mustard, brown sugar and cocoa in it. Return to the meat mixture and simmer again. Baste the meat balls with the sauce so that they will be evenly flavored. If you like a sweet-sour mustard sauce, add 1 tablespoon cider vinegar just before serving.

Serve with plain boiled potatoes or with boiled rice. This also goes well with buttered noodles.

CHICK PEAS AND MEAT BALLS

1 pound (approximately) soup bone
4 strips lean bacon, cut into ¼" pieces
3 cups water
1 cup dried chick peas, soaked overnight in 3 cups water
1 stalk leek, cut into fine pieces
1 large carrot, cut into ⅛" slices
2 medium-sized raw potatoes, scrubbed but not peeled, diced in ½" pieces
1 pound hamburger
1 small green pepper, chopped very fine
1 small onion, chopped very fine
½ teaspoon salt
¼ teaspoon pepper
2 eggs, beaten until they are lemon yellow

Place the soup bone and bacon in the water and bring to a rolling boil. Drain the soaked chick peas and add them. Skim the froth from time to time as it rises to the top. Boil for 1 hour, or until the chick peas are tender. Remove the soup bone and discard. Add the leek, carrot, and raw potatoes. Simmer for an additional 30 minutes.

Meanwhile, mix the hamburger, green pepper, onion, salt, pepper and eggs very well. Form into meat balls about the size of golf balls and drop into the simmering chick pea mixture. Simmer for 30 minutes longer. Turn the mixture from time to time to keep it from sticking to the bottom of the pan and to insure even cooking of the meat balls.

Serve in a large tureen, garnished with paprika.

SWEDISH MEAT BALLS

½ cup soft bread crumbs
½ cup light sweet cream
¼ pound ground veal
¼ pound pork (can be fat)
1 pound ground beef
1 tablespoon onion juice
1 teaspoon salt
¼ teaspoon nutmeg
4 twists of pepper mill
½ teaspoon white sugar
1 tablespoon melted butter
2 tablespoons butter for frying

Soak the bread crumbs in the cream. Meanwhile, mix all of the meat together very well. Add the onion juice, salt, nutmeg, pepper and sugar. Finally stir the melted butter into the milk-bread crumb mixture.

Using the large end of a melon-ball maker, form the meat mixture into little balls and place in a skillet in the butter. From time to time, shake the skillet back and forth to brown the meat balls on all sides. This shaking action will brown them more evenly than turning them over with a spatula.

This is a dish that can be served either hot or cold.

SWEDISH MEAT BALLS #2

½ cup bread crumbs
1 tablespoon onion flakes
½ cup milk
1 pound ground chuck
1 teaspoon salt
4 twists of pepper mill
⅛ teaspoon ginger
¼ teaspoon nutmeg
5 tablespoons cream cheese (softened at room temperature)
2 tablespoons butter or margarine
1 can cream of mushroom soup

Soak the bread crumbs and onion flakes in the milk. Meanwhile, mix the meat with the salt, pepper, ginger and nutmeg. Add the milk, onion and bread crumb mixture to the meat and stir lightly. Last, stir in the cream cheese.

Using the large end of a melon-ball maker, form into little meat balls and place in a skillet with the melted butter. Shake the pan back and forth while browning. This will keep the meat balls nice and round. After all of the meat balls have become golden brown, pour the mushroom soup over them. Turn the heat down to a very low simmer until the soup is all melted and thoroughly distributed.

Serve with plain boiled potatoes.

SWEDISH MEAT BALLS #3

1 pound ground chuck
1 pound ground lean pork
2 eggs, beaten to a lemon yellow
1 cup bread crumbs
¾ cup mashed potatoes
1 teaspoon salt
1 cup condensed milk
1 teaspoon brown sugar
¼ teaspoon cloves
¼ teaspoon ginger
¼ teaspoon nutmeg
¼ teaspoon allspice
4 twists of pepper mill
3 tablespoons butter for frying
2 cups half and half cream

Mix very well all of the ingredients—except the butter for frying and the cream—in the order in which they are listed. Using the large end of a melon-ball maker, form into tiny meat balls. Sauté the meat balls in the butter until they are well browned. Shake the pan from side to side so that they roll and brown evenly on all sides. Pour off any excess drippings which may accumulate during the frying. Stir in the cream and simmer for 20 minutes, or until the sauce is thickened.

Serve with boiled potatoes or with broad noodles.

MEAT BALLS WITH SWEET AND SOUR MUSHROOMS

Meat balls

1 pound ground chuck
1 egg
½ teaspoon salt
¼ teaspoon pepper
½ cup soft bread crumbs
¼ cup milk
3 tablespoons butter

Mushroom sauce

3 cups small fresh mushrooms
1 tablespoon flour
1 10½-ounce can beef consommé
1 tablespoon sugar
Juice of 1 lemon

Thoroughly mix all the meat ball ingredients except the butter and form into balls about 1″ in diameter. Using a large skillet, melt the butter and place the meat balls in it. To brown them evenly, gently shake the pan back and forth so that they roll and turn. When all are evenly browned, remove them from the skillet to a platter and make the sauce.

Clean the mushrooms under running water, and drain. Stir the flour into the butter left in the skillet. When it is blended, add the consommé. Cook for 5 minutes over moderate heat until thickened. Add the sugar and lemon juice. Stir in the mushrooms, being careful not to break them. Simmer for 10 minutes, turning frequently so that the mushrooms are all coated and tender. Add the meat balls and simmer for 5 minutes longer.

Arrange on a heated platter, garnished with parsley. If you want an especially festive dish, sprinkle toasted chopped almonds and pimento over the top.

DUTCH KLOPSE

1 pound ground lean pork
1 pound ground lean veal
2 eggs
½ cup moist bread crumbs
½ teaspoon salt
4 twists of pepper mill
2 quarts water
2 tablespoons cider vinegar
1 teaspoon mixed pickling spices
4 tablespoons butter or margarine
3 tablespoons flour
3 cups meat stock or 3 cups water with 6 bouillon cubes
   dissolved in it
1 tablespoon capers

Mix the pork and veal, eggs and bread crumbs together.
Add the salt and pepper. Bring the water to a rolling boil;
add the vinegar and spices. Form the meat into balls about
the size of golf balls and drop one by one into the boiling
water. Cover and simmer for 10 minutes.

Melt the butter in a deep skillet and stir in the flour until
it is smooth. Add the meat stock and stir until it is thickened.
Remove the meat balls from the boiling spiced water and
put them into the thickened sauce. Add the capers and simmer
for 15 minutes longer.

Serve piping hot with plain boiled potatoes.

MEAT BALLS WITH PINE NUTS

1 pound hamburger
1 cup mashed potatoes
¼ cup pine nuts
1 tablespoon dried black currants
¼ teaspoon thyme
¼ teaspoon dill seeds
1 tablespoon dehydrated parsley
½ teaspoon salt
4 twists of pepper mill
Oil for deep frying

Mix all of the ingredients very thoroughly. Form into meat
balls about the size of golf balls. Drop into deep-frying oil
one at a time and fry until they are golden brown. Remove to
paper toweling to drain. Serve with chili sauce or catsup.

HAMBURGER SHISH KABOBS

1 pound ground round steak
½ cup mild Cheddar cheese, grated
1 teaspoon salt
1 teaspoon garlic powder
¼ teaspoon pepper
½ teaspoon cinnamon
1 #2 can small potatoes
8 cherry tomatoes or 4 very small tomatoes, halved
1 #2 can boiled onions
2 green peppers, sliced in 4 pieces the long way

Mix the ground meat, cheese, salt, garlic powder, pepper and cinnamon very well. Form into 16 meat balls about 1½" in diameter.

On shish kabob skewers put a potato first, then a meat ball, then a cherry tomato or tomato wedge, then an onion, another meat ball, and last a piece of green pepper, folded in half. Repeat until all the ingredients are used up. Place on a broiling rack under the broiler and cook until the meat is browned on all sides. Serve immediately.

WESTERN-STYLE MEAT BALLS

¾ cup quick-cooking oatmeal
½ pound ground chuck, mixed with ½ pound ground veal
   (if possible, have the butcher put the meat through the
   grinder two or three times)
1 teaspoon salt
4 twists of pepper mill
¾ cup condensed milk
3 tablespoons flour
1 teaspoon paprika
3 tablespoons olive oil
½ cup onion, diced into ¼" pieces
¼ cup barbecue sauce
1 can condensed tomato soup
1 soup can water
1 package frozen niblet-style corn

Mix the oatmeal with the ground meat, add the salt, pepper and milk. Form into meat balls about the size of golf balls. Mix the flour and paprika thoroughly, and roll each of the meat balls in this mixture until they are coated on all sides.

Heat the olive oil in a deep skillet with a tight-fitting cover. Sauté the meat balls until they are a rich brown. Add the onion, and continue to cook until it is transparent. Drain off any excess oil left in the pan.

Mix the barbecue sauce with the tomato soup and water. Pour this sauce over the meat balls and let simmer, tightly covered, for 30 minutes. Spoon the sauce over the meat balls from time to time during this period.

Break up the frozen corn and add to the meat balls. Simmer for 10 minutes longer. Serve immediately, piping hot.

NOTE: Lima beans, baked beans, French-style green beans, black-eyed peas or frozen succotash may be used for variety instead of the corn.

MEAT BALLS WITH CORN AND BEANS

2 pounds hamburger
1 teaspoon monosodium glutamate
1 teaspoon salt
¼ teaspoon pepper
1 egg, slightly beaten
2 tablespoons butter or margarine
¼ cup chopped onion
2 cloves of garlic, minced very fine, or 1 tablespoon garlic juice
½ teaspoon chili powder
1 #2 can niblet-style corn
1 #2 can red kidney beans, not drained
1 cup canned tomatoes

Mix the hamburger with the monosodium glutamate, salt, pepper and egg. Dipping your hands in cold water, form this mixture into meat balls about the size of golf balls. Melt the butter in a large skillet; add the onion and garlic. Cook for 5 minutes and then add the meat balls. Sprinkle the chili powder over the meat balls; continue to sauté the meat balls until they are well browned. Drain off any excess grease after they are done.

Place the browned meat balls in the bottom of a 1½-quart casserole. Mix the corn, kidney beans and tomatoes together and pour over the meat balls. Place in a 375° F. oven for 25 minutes. Serve piping hot.

Chapter X

LAMBURGERS

LAMB has long been a favorite of Middle Eastern peoples. Here in the United States it is not used as much as it should be, which is unfortunate, because it is a meat that is high in protein and low in fat.

Most supermarkets now have lamb patties made up in packages of four, six or eight. Occasionally you can convince the butcher to sell you a pound of ground lamb not made up into patties. If you can't get it ground by the pound, buy the patties; it takes little effort to break them up and use them instead. Besides, since a leg of spring lamb rivals porterhouse steak in price most of the time, getting the patties may be less expensive than having a whole piece ground for yourself. The patties are usually about equal in price to ground chuck.

Many people say they dislike lamb because, without being aware of it, they were once served mutton when they thought they were getting lamb—and mutton is a very tasteless meat. Today, however, when a package is labeled lamb, it is truly lamb.

If there is anyone in your household who claims he dislikes lamb, sneak in one of the following recipes. You may make a convert to the cause of this nutritious and healthful food.

LAMB SOUP

1 pound ground lamb
1 medium-sized onion, sliced very thin
1 box frozen shredded spinach
¼ cup chopped parsley
¼ teaspoon paprika
3 cups water
¼ cup precooked rice
1 teaspoon salt
¼ teaspoon pepper
1 egg yolk
1 cup sour cream

Put the ground lamb into a soup kettle over a low flame. Sauté slowly until the lamb is golden brown. Drain off any accumulation of fat. Add the onion and the frozen spinach and cook, uncovered, for 5 minutes more, or until the spinach is thawed and separated. Add the parsley, paprika, water and rice. Add the salt and pepper; bring to a rolling boil and then turn the heat down to simmer. Simmer for 10 minutes.

Beat the egg yolk until it is lemon yellow; add the sour cream and beat together until very smooth. Remove the soup from the stove. Stir several spoonfuls of the hot soup into the sour cream and egg and then add the cream and egg mixture to the soup. Cook for a few seconds longer before serving.

Garnish with sprigs of parsley if you wish additional color.

LAMB PILAF

3 tablespoons butter or margarine
1 pound ground lamb
1 onion, diced
2 tablespoons dried black currants
1 tablespoon pine nuts (optional)
1 tablespoon dehydrated parsley
¼ teaspoon allspice
2 cups precooked rice
1 teaspoon salt
¼ teaspoon pepper
1 cup canned tomatoes
2 cups meat stock or 2 cups warm water with 4 bouillon cubes dissolved in it

Place the butter or margarine in the bottom of a kettle which has a tight-fitting cover. Melt, and brown the ground lamb in it. Add the onion, and continue to cook until it is transparent. Add the black currants, pine nuts, parsley, allspice and rice. Continue to cook for 8 minutes longer. Stir constantly so that there is no scorching or sticking. Add the salt and pepper, the tomatoes and meat stock. Stir all very well.

Cook over low heat for about 20 minutes. At this point all of the liquid should have been absorbed by the rice. If there is still too much, turn the heat down to simmer, take off the cover of the kettle and place a clean dish towel (folded in two thicknesses) over the opening of the kettle. Replace the cover on top of the towel and cook for 5 minutes longer. The towel will absorb all of the unwanted liquid and leave the rice in beautiful separate grains.

Serve on a hot platter.

LAMB-EGGPLANT CASSEROLE

If you mention lamb and eggplant to anyone of Turkish or Greek extraction, they light up like a neon sign and start describing how delicious it is. Try it!

1 pound ground lamb
2 tablespoons olive oil
4 medium-sized onions, chopped fine
¼ cup parsley
1 teaspoon monosodium glutamate
½ teaspoon salt
¼ teaspoon pepper
2 eggs, separated
1 cup soft bread crumbs
4 cups whole milk
6 tablespoons cornstarch
1 2-pound eggplant, or 2 smaller ones, peeled and cut in ½" slices
6 tablespoons olive oil for frying
½ cup Parmesan or Parmesan-Romano cheese

Sauté the lamb in the olive oil until golden brown. Add the onions, parsley, monosodium glutamate, salt and pepper and continue to cook for 5 minutes longer. Beat the egg whites until they stand in peaks. Fold in the bread crumbs. Remove the meat mixture from the stove and set aside to cool. When cool, fold in the egg white and bread crumb mixture.

In the top of your double boiler, mix the milk with the cornstarch and cook over rapidly boiling water until it coats the spoon. Stir frequently during cooking. Beat the egg yolks until light. Add a few spoonfuls of the thickened white sauce to the egg yolks. Then add the egg yolks to the white sauce. (This prevents curdling.) Cook for 3 minutes longer.

Heat the olive oil in a large skillet and gently fry the eggplant slices until they are slightly browned. Into a greased 1½-quart casserole, place a layer of the browned eggplant. Follow this with half of the meat mixture. Place another layer of eggplant over this and follow with half of the cream sauce. Now place remainder of the meat mixture over the cream sauce and follow with another layer of eggplant. Pour the remainder of the cream sauce over the entire casserole, and sprinkle with the cheese. Place in a 425° F. oven for 45 minutes.

LAMB IN GRAPE LEAVES

This is a famous Greek delicacy, time consuming to make but wonderful to eat. It is used in most Greek households for festive occasions; try it for one of your special dinners.

½ pound ground lamb
½ cup rice
2 onions, chopped very fine
5 tablespoons olive oil
1 can beef bouillon
1 teaspoon Accent
½ teaspoon salt
¼ teaspoon pepper
40 grape leaves*
6 tablespoons butter

Put the lamb into a skillet over low heat and sauté until it is golden brown. Add the rice, onions and olive oil. Continue to sauté until the rice kernels turn snow white. Add the bouillon, Accent, salt and pepper. Simmer until the rice has absorbed all of the liquid.

If using fresh grape leaves, wash them thoroughly in warm water, then plunge into boiling water for a few seconds. Drain the leaves and place a tablespoonful of the meat-rice mixture in the center of each leaf. Roll the leaf up tightly, folding in the ends as you would do when wrapping a package. Place the grape leaf rolls side by side in the bottom of a heavy saucepan. Additional leaves go between the layers. Dot the tops of the rolled-up leaves with pieces of butter, and add enough water to cover. Cover the saucepan tightly and simmer for 1½ hours. Serve with Egg-Lemon Sauce, below.

Egg-Lemon Sauce

2 eggs
Juice of 2 lemons

Drain the excess liquid from the saucepan containing the grape leaves and set them aside to cool slightly. Beat the eggs until they are lemon colored. While still beating, add the lemon juice and the liquid from the grape leaf-lamb mixture. Pour this sauce over the grape leaves, and serve.

* If you know anyone who grows grapes, you may be able to get leaves fresh from the vine. But be careful; some grape leaves are too harsh in flavor to be palatable. If fresh leaves are unobtainable, prepared ones may be purchased in any international food store.

LAMB AND RICE

1½ pounds ground lamb
1 medium onion, sliced thin
1 #2 can tomato juice
1½ cups uncooked rice
1 teaspoon Accent
½ teaspoon salt
¼ teaspoon pepper
⅛ teaspoon cinnamon
⅛ teaspoon nutmeg

Brown the ground lamb in the bottom of a large kettle. Pour off any accumulated fat. Add the onion and cook until it is slightly glazed. Add the tomato juice and rice, then the Accent, salt, pepper, cinnamon and nutmeg. Stir all together thoroughly.

If there is not enough liquid to cover, add some warm water. Simmer slowly for 20 minutes. When cooking is done, the rice should be doubled in size. If any liquid remains, cook without a cover for a few minutes until the liquid disappears.

GYPSY LAMB STEW

1 pound ground lamb
3 carrots, peeled and sliced very thin
3 onions, sliced very thin
⅛ teaspoon aniseed
½ teaspoon salt
¼ teaspoon pepper
2 cups precooked rice
2 cups water
4 shallots (green onions), sliced very thin
1 green pepper, diced into ¼″ pieces

Place the ground lamb in a 2-quart kettle which has a tight-fitting cover. Brown the lamb until it is all broken apart and a golden brown in color. Add the carrots and onions, and continue to cook until the onion slices are clear and transparent. Add the aniseed, salt and pepper and mix well.

Place the rice over the lamb mixture and cover with the water. With cover on kettle, cook over low heat until all of the liquid is absorbed and the rice is fluffy. Mix lightly before placing on a heated platter. Garnish with the shallots and green pepper.

LAMB STEW, TURKISH STYLE

1½ pounds ground lamb
1 tablespoon olive oil
4 large potatoes, peeled and diced
6 small onions
2 green peppers, seeded and sliced in rings
4 cloves garlic, sliced very thin
1 bay leaf
1 teaspoon sage leaves or ½ teaspoon ground sage
1 teaspoon fennel, chopped very fine (optional)
1 teaspoon dill seed
1 #2 can tomatoes
2 cups meat stock or 2 cups warm water with 4 bouillon
    cubes dissolved in it
1 tablespoon flour

Place the lamb and olive oil in a large cooking kettle.
Brown the lamb until it is all separated. Add the potatoes, onions, peppers, garlic, bay leaf, sage, fennel (if you want to
use it) and dill seed. Last, stir in the tomatoes and meat stock.
Cover tightly and simmer for 1 hour.

Just before serving, remove ½ cup of the gravy, let cool,
and stir in the flour. Return this flour-gravy mixture to the
kettle and stir until the stew is thickened.

OKRA WITH LAMB

1 pound ground lamb
1 onion, chopped fine
½ cup water
½ teaspoon salt
¼ teaspoon pepper
¾ cup canned tomato sauce
½ cup rice
2 packages frozen okra

Brown the lamb in the bottom of a kettle with a tight-fitting
cover. Pour off any grease accumulation after the lamb has
browned. Add the onion, water, salt, pepper and tomato sauce.
Bring to a boil.

Stir in the rice and okra. Simmer over a very low flame for
45 minutes with the cover on tight. If at the end of this time
there is still moisture, continue to cook for a few minutes
longer without the cover.

Garnish with very thin slices of lemon, if desired.

LAMB WITH POMEGRANATES

1 pound ground lamb
1 egg
1 tablespoon minced or instant onion
½ teaspoon salt
1 teaspoon Accent
⅛ teaspoon thyme
¼ teaspoon pepper
½ cup moist bread crumbs
1 tablespoon butter or margarine
2 large pomegranates
1 cup water
2 cups instant rice

Mix the lamb with the egg, onion, salt, Accent, thyme, pepper and bread crumbs. Form into meat patties about 3″ in diameter and ¾″ thick. Melt the butter or margarine in a large skillet and brown the lamb patties until they are golden brown.

Peel the pomegranates and remove all the fibrous pith. Put the pulp into a chopping bowl and chop until very fine. Add this to the lamb; then add the water. Cover and cook over low heat for 25 minutes. Turn the patties several times during the cooking so that the pomegranate flavor is evenly distributed.

Cook the rice according to the directions on the package and serve with the meat balls and gravy poured over.

LAMBURGERS WITH EGGPLANT

1 pound ground lamb
½ teaspoon salt
¼ teaspoon pepper
¼ cup olive oil
4 large onions, sliced
1 medium-sized eggplant
1 cup stock or 1 10½-ounce can consommé
1 #2 can tomatoes
2 eggs
¼ cup milk

Season the ground lamb with the salt and pepper. Put the olive oil in a skillet and sauté the lamb in it until it is golden brown and all broken apart. Strain the lamb from the olive oil and set aside. Slice the eggplant in ½″ slices; do not peel. Sauté the eggplant in the olive oil until it begins to brown. Then remove from the olive oil and set aside.

Pour the olive oil left in the skillet into a large baking dish; swirl it around so that it will coat the sides and bottom. Place a layer of the eggplant on the bottom. Follow this with a layer of meat, and then a layer of the sliced onions. Repeat until all the ingredients are used up.

Mix the stock with the tomatoes and pour over the ingredients in the baking dish. Cover and bake in a 350° F. oven for 35 minutes. The liquid should be reduced to half by this time; if it is not, bake for a few minutes longer without a cover.

Beat the eggs until they are lemon colored, add the milk and beat again. Pour this over the lamb and eggplant. Reduce the oven heat to 250° F. and bake for an additional 35 minutes, or until the eggs have formed a custard on top of the dish. Serve piping hot.

LAMB CAKES

1 pound ground lamb
½ cup cooked rice
1 tablespoon dehydrated onion
1 tablespoon dehydrated parsley
½ teaspoon celery seed
½ teaspoon salt
4 twists of pepper mill
1 teaspoon dried mint leaves, crushed
2 eggs
½ cup flour
1 teaspoon water
Deep fat for frying

Mix the lamb, rice, onion, parsley, celery seed, salt, pepper and mint leaves very thoroughly. Set aside while you prepare the following dough:

Break the eggs into the flour, add the water, and knead and work until you have a stiff dough. If the eggs are large you may have to add a little more flour. On a floured pastry cloth, roll out the dough until it is about 1/16″ thick. With a tumbler or round cookie cutter, cut circles. Place a tablespoonful of the lamb mixture in the center of half the circles, then place another circle on top of each. Press the edges tightly to seal each double circle.

Meanwhile, heat the frying oil to 350° F. Drop in each little cake individually. As soon as each is golden brown, remove it and place it in a warm oven until the others are fried. These cakes are delicious served with a salad. They can also be prepared in advance and refrigerated or frozen.

LAMBURGERS WITH LEMON SAUCE

4 large carrots
2 stalks celery
2 large onions
½ teaspoon salt
¼ teaspoon pepper
2 pounds ground lamb
1 egg (for the meat balls)
2 tablespoons flour
3 egg yolks
1 tablespoon cold water
⅓ cup fresh lemon juice

Chop the carrots, celery and onions until they are about the consistency of cole slaw. Cover with water and place over low heat to simmer. Add the salt and pepper to the lamb; stir in the unbeaten egg; mix very well. Dipping hands in cold water, form into meat balls about the size of a walnut.

When the vegetables have simmered so that the celery and onions are clear and transparent, drop in the meat balls one at a time. Raise the heat if necessary so that the balls will not lose their shape upon contact with the liquid. Continue to simmer for 30 minutes.

Drain the liquid from the meat balls and vegetables and place them on a heated platter in a 200° F. oven. Take 2 tablespoons of the liquid and stir the flour into it until it is a smooth paste; gradually stir the flour mixture into the remainder of the meat-vegetable liquid. Cook until it is thickened.

Beat the egg yolks until they are lemon colored; gradually add the water and the lemon juice and continue to beat until frothy. Pour into the thickened sauce very gradually; stir constantly while adding. Remove from the heat and pour over the meat balls and vegetables.

Serve with plain boiled potatoes.

LAMB SHISH KABOBS

Meat Balls

2 pounds ground lamb
2 eggs, well beaten
2 cloves garlic or 1 tablespoon garlic juice
1 teaspoon salt
¼ teaspoon pepper

Marinade

2 tablespoons grated onion
1 tablespoon vinegar
Juice of 1 lemon
1 teaspoon grated lemon rind
¼ teaspoon cloves
2 bay leaves
½ cup water
½ cup red wine (preferably Burgundy)

Accompaniments

1 #2 can boiled potatoes, drained
1 #2 can boiled onions, drained
4 tomatoes, cut into wedges
2 green peppers, sliced lengthwise

Mix the lamb with the eggs, garlic, salt and pepper. Form into 1½″ meat balls. Have a kettle of boiling water ready; as you finish each meat ball, drop it into the boiling water for a few seconds. This will make the meat balls firm enough to put on the skewers.

Put all of the marinade ingredients except the wine in a small saucepan. Bring to a boil and remove from stove to cool. Then add the wine. Strain the marinade into a shallow dish large enough to hold all the meat balls. Add the meat balls to the marinade and roll them back and forth gently so that they all become well coated. Let them stand in the marinade in a cool place for 1 hour.

Slip a meat ball on the skewer; follow with a potato, an onion, a tomato and a slice of green pepper, folded in half. Repeat until all of the ingredients are used up. Place skewers on a broiling rack and broil. Turn during the broiling so that all the meat is evenly browned. Serve immediately.

LAMBURGERS WITH FRESH CRANBERRIES

2 pounds ground lamb
1 egg, beaten slightly
½ teaspoon salt
4 twists of pepper mill
⅛ teaspoon rosemary
2 cups fresh cranberries
½ cup sugar
2 tablespoons lemon juice
1 teaspoon grated lemon rind
1 small onion, minced
2 cups precooked rice
2 cups water

Mix the ground lamb with the egg, salt, pepper and rosemary. Form into 8 patties, and sauté in a deep skillet until they are brown on both sides. Drain off any excess drippings.

In a separate saucepan place the cranberries, sugar, lemon juice, lemon rind and onion. Cook over low heat until the cranberries are tender. Add this mixture to the lamb patties and simmer for 8 minutes longer.

Bring the water to a boil and add the rice. Cook for 5 minutes or until all the kernels are separated and tender. Place the hot rice on a platter and top with the lamb patty-cranberry mixture.

LAMBURGERS, INDIAN STYLE

1½ pounds ground lamb
1 teaspoon salt
1 tablespoon olive oil
2 onions, cut into ⅛" slices
¼ teaspoon cumin
¼ teaspoon ginger
¼ teaspoon paprika
½ teaspoon coriander
¼ teaspoon tumeric
¼ teaspoon nutmeg
1 #2 can tomatoes
½ cup sour cream

Mix the ground lamb and the salt thoroughly. Form into 2" diameter meat patties, and brown in the olive oil until a rich deep brown. Turn down the heat and add the onions, all of the spices and the tomatoes. Simmer for 45 minutes. Cover during this time.

Stir 2 tablespoons of the gravy from the meat balls into the sour cream, then mix the sour cream with the rest of the gravy. Simmer for an additional 8 minutes. Turn the meat patties over from time to time so that they are all coated with the gravy. Serve with noodles, rice or riced potatoes.

PATLIJAN A LA NAZ

2 medium-sized eggplants
2 tablespoons salt
1 pound ground lamb
½ cup chopped parsley
½ teaspoon salt
¼ teaspoon pepper
10 slices onion ¼″ thick
5 slices bacon, cut in half
1 #2 can tomatoes

Do not peel the eggplants. Cut 1″ off the bottom and the top and discard. Cut each eggplant into 5 uniform slices. Place the eggplant slices in a shallow dish and sprinkle with the salt. Let stand for at least 1 hour, or until the slices are soft.

Mix the lamb with the parsley, salt and pepper. Form into 10 uniform patties about the same size as the eggplant slices. Drain the water accumulation from the eggplant. Wipe each slice with a cloth and then place in a flat greased baking dish. On top of each slice of eggplant put a slice of onion. Place a lamb patty on top of the onion. Press down the edges on the eggplant. Put a half slice of bacon over each lamb patty. Distribute the tomatoes and their juice around the eggplant-lamb rings. Bake in a 350° F. oven for 1 hour and 45 minutes.

Chapter XI

VIVA ITALIA

THE UNITED STATES owes Italy many debts of gratitude. Among other things, they have sent us wonderful people, wonderful music—and wonderful food. Every American housewife has at least one prized recipe for a macaroni dish; and the impact pizza has had on American eating habits is a phenomenon of the postwar period.

Most Italian recipes feature *pasta*, or macaroni, a generic term which includes spaghetti and noodles as well as many different varieties of macaroni itself. By last count there were about 160 types of macaroni. Naturally even the larger supermarkets do not handle them all; they feature only the types that are most popular. If you want to go all out for Italian cooking, and need the more unusual shapes of macaroni, you can probably find them in an Italian specialty store.

Cooking macaroni is an art. Nothing in the world can ruin a good Italian dish more than overcooked macaroni. You should use 3 quarts of slightly salted water to each half pound of macaroni. Have the water boiling rapidly before adding the macaroni; boil for 5 minutes, and then start testing. The macaroni should be firm when you bite it. Naturally, the thinner the shape of the particular variety of macaroni you are using, the shorter the cooking time. For instance, spaghettini (thin spaghetti) will require less cooking time than a heavier kind of *pasta*.

Many cooks ruin good macaroni by rinsing it in cold water after cooking. Never, never do this. The macaroni will get chilled, and when you mix it with the sauce there will be a congealing action that will destroy the flavor of the whole dish. If you want to stop the cooking action, pour a cup or two of cold water into the boiling macaroni. Then drain at once and cover with the proper sauce.

RICE, HAMBURGER AND ZUCCHINI

1 tablespoon olive oil
1 pound ground chuck
1 small onion, chopped very fine
3 potatoes, peeled and diced
4 medium zucchini squash, cut in ¼" slices
2 stalks celery, sliced fine
2 cups precooked rice
2 cups water
1 #2 can kidney beans, drained
½ cup Parmesan cheese

Put the olive oil in a deep saucepan with a tight-fitting cover. Sauté the ground meat until it is brown, then add the onion, potatoes, squash and celery. Cover tightly and cook for 8 minutes, or until the potatoes are done. Add the rice and the water; stir so that all is well mixed. Cover tightly and place over low heat for 8 minutes. Then remove from the heat and stir in the kidney beans. Set aside for 5 minutes. There will be enough heat in the rice mixture to heat the beans.

Place on a heated platter and sprinkle the cheese over the top. Serve immediately.

ITALIAN RICE

3 tablespoons butter
½ pound ground chuck
1 tablespoon dehydrated onion
2 cups precooked rice
2 cups beef bouillon
Pinch of saffron
½ teaspoon salt
¼ teaspoon pepper
Butter for dotting
½ cup Parmesan cheese

Place the 3 tablespoons of butter in the bottom of a deep saucepan with a tight-fitting cover. Melt the butter and add the meat. Sauté until the meat is brown. Add the onion, and stir in the rice just as it comes from the package. Cook, uncovered, for 5 minutes.

Add the bouillon, saffron, salt and pepper. Turn the heat to low and cook, covered, for 5 minutes, or until all the liquid is absorbed. Put the rice and meat on a hot platter, dot with a little butter and sprinkle the cheese over the top.

Serve piping hot, garnished with sprigs of parsley.

HAMBURGER SCALLOPINE

1 pound ground chuck
1 pound ground veal
1 egg, slightly beaten
½ cup bread crumbs
½ teaspoon salt
¼ teaspoon nutmeg
1 teaspoon sugar
¼ teaspoon pepper
1 tablespoon paprika
2 tablespoons butter or margarine
1 clove garlic, minced
2 medium-sized onions, sliced
1 4-ounce can mushroom stems and pieces
Juice of 1 lemon
1 8-ounce can tomato sauce
1 teaspoon dry mustard
¼ teaspoon thyme
2 tablespoons parsley, chopped

Mix the chuck and veal; add the slightly beaten egg and the bread crumbs. Add the salt, nutmeg, sugar and pepper. Mix all very well. Form into 8 meat patties. Sprinkle each side of the patties with paprika. Melt the butter in a large skillet. Brown the meat patties on each side. Then add the garlic, onions and mushrooms; continue to cook until the onions are glazed and transparent.

Mix the lemon juice with the tomato sauce; add the mustard and thyme. Pour the sauce over the meat patties and cook for 35 minutes. Keep the skillet covered during this period. If the sauce gets too thick, add a little water from time to time.

Garnish with the parsley and serve with boiled potatoes.

MACARONI AND MEAT BALLS

3 tablespoons butter
1 pound ground chuck
1 tablespoon dehydrated onion
3 tablespoons flour
1½ cups milk
½ teaspoon salt
¼ teaspoon nutmeg
3 tablespoons Parmesan-Romano cheese
2 egg yolks, beaten with 1 tablespoon water
1 8-ounce package elbow macaroni
3 quarts rapidly boiling slightly salted water

Melt the butter in a skillet; add the ground meat and the dehydrated onion. Cook until the meat is slightly browned and well separated. Remove the meat from the butter by straining it. Return the butter to the skillet.

Over very low heat, add the flour to the butter and stir until it is smooth. Add the milk, salt and nutmeg. Cook over low heat, stirring constantly until it is thick. This should be a rather heavy-bodied cream sauce. Remove from the heat and allow to cool. Then stir in the egg yolks and cheese. Add the browned meat to the sauce.

Put the macaroni in the water. Cook for 10 minutes, or until tender. Drain and place in a greased casserole dish. Pour the meat sauce over the macaroni and place in a 350° F. oven for 20 minutes. Serve immediately.

PIZZA WITH HAMBURGER

1 pound hamburger
1 onion, cut into ¼" slices
1 can tomato paste
2 tablespoons water
½ teaspoon salt
¼ teaspoon pepper
½ teaspoon oregano

Dough

2 cups biscuit mix
¾ cup milk
⅛ teaspoon salt
½ cup grated Parmesan cheese
2 tablespoons olive oil

Mix the hamburger with the onion, tomato paste, water, salt, pepper and oregano. Set aside for a few minutes to allow flavors to blend.

Mix the biscuit dough with the milk and ⅛ teaspoon salt. Divide the dough in half. On a floured board, roll out the 2 pieces of dough large enough to fit 9" cake tins. Grease the cake tins, place the dough in them and cover the tops with forkfuls of the meat mixture. Sprinkle the cheese over the top, and sprinkle a tablespoonful of olive oil on each pie. Bake in a preheated 400° F. oven for 25 minutes, or until the crust is golden brown. Serve piping hot.

LASAGNE #1

2 tablespoons olive oil
1 pound ground chuck
½ cup minced onion
1 #2 can tomatoes
1 6-ounce can tomato paste
1 cup water
½ teaspoon salt
¼ teaspoon pepper
1 teaspoon light brown sugar
1 pound lasagne
6 quarts rapidly boiling slightly salted water
1 cup large-curd creamed cottage cheese
6 3″ slices mozzarella cheese, cut into 1″ squares
½ cup grated Parmesan cheese

Place the olive oil in the bottom of a deep kettle with a tight-fitting cover. Heat oil and add the chuck. Sauté until the meat is brown and well separated. Add the onion and continue to cook until it becomes transparent. Add the tomatoes, tomato paste, water, salt, pepper and sugar. Stir all very well and bring to a simmer. Let simmer for 35 minutes. Stir from time to time to prevent any sticking to the bottom of the pan.

Meanwhile, cook the lasagne in the 6 quarts of water for about 15 minutes, or until you can break off a piece of the lasagne with the side of a fork. Remove from heat and drain. Allow to cool. Grease an oblong, 3″ deep baking dish. Remove meat sauce from stove. Allow to cool.

Cover the bottom of the baking dish with a couple of spoonfuls of the meat sauce; top with strips of lasagne. Place 3 or 4 tablespoonfuls of the cottage cheese on next; distribute a few squares of the mozzarella, sprinkle on a little of the Parmesan. Now add 3 more tablespoonfuls of the meat sauce. Cover with a layer of lasagne, and continue layering in the same sequence until all the ingredients are used up. The final layer should be meat sauce.

Place the baking dish, uncovered, in a 350° F. oven for 40 minutes. After removing from oven, allow lasagne to cool for at least 15 minutes; otherwise all the layers will run together.

This dish can be made ahead of time and reheated by placing in a 350° F. oven for 30 minutes. It freezes well, too.

LASAGNE #2

1 pound Italian sausage
1 pound ground chuck
1 clove garlic, minced
½ teaspoon sweet basil
2 large onions, diced
2 stalks celery, diced
1 10½-ounce can minestrone soup
1 6-ounce can tomato paste
1½ cups water
½ teaspoon salt
¼ teaspoon pepper
1 pound lasagne
6 quarts rapidly boiling slightly salted water
½ pound white goat's milk cheese (cream style), or substitute ½ pound large-curd creamed cottage cheese, broken up
1 cup grated Parmesan cheese

Remove the casings from the sausage and place it in a deep kettle. Sauté the sausage meat until it is golden brown; then add the chuck. Cook together until the chuck loses its reddish color. Add the garlic, basil, onions and celery and continue to cook until the onion is transparent. Add the soup, tomato paste, water, salt and pepper. Simmer for 30 minutes.

Meanwhile, cook the lasagne in the water until it is tender enough for you to cut it against the side of the kettle with a fork. Remove from the heat and drain, but do not rinse.

Place a layer of lasagne over the bottom of a large rectangular buttered baking dish about 3" deep. On this sprinkle 2 tablespoonfuls of each cheese. Add a few spoonfuls of the hot meat sauce, then another layer of lasagne. Continue to repeat these layers until you have used up all of the lasagne. End with meat sauce on top; do not top with lasagne or the top layer will become tough in the baking.

Place in a 350° F. oven for 40 minutes. Remove from the oven and let cool for at least 15 minutes so that the cheese can set firmly. Cut into squares and serve.

HAMBURGER AND RICE WITH ARTICHOKES

3 tablespoons butter
½ pound ground chuck
½ pound Italian sausage
1 large onion, chopped very fine
1 8-ounce can mushroom stems and pieces
1 package frozen artichoke hearts
1 package frozen peas
1 tablespoon dehydrated parsley
½ teaspoon salt
¼ teaspoon pepper
1 cup precooked rice
1 can chicken gumbo soup
1 soup can water
½ cup buttered bread crumbs
½ cup Parmesan cheese

Melt the butter in a deep kettle with a tight-fitting cover. Add the ground meat and the sausage, after removing its casings. Sauté until the meat is golden brown. Add the onion, mushrooms, artichoke hearts, peas, parsley, salt and pepper Cover and simmer for 8 minutes. Remove from heat.

Stir in the rice, soup and water. Place all in a greased casserole and cover with aluminum foil. Bake in a 375° F. oven for 20 minutes. All the liquid should be absorbed by this time. If it is not, return the casserole to the oven for a few minutes longer.

Mix the bread crumbs and the cheese together. Remove the foil from the casserole and sprinkle the bread crumbs and cheese over the top. Return to the oven for 5 minutes longer, or until the bread crumb and cheese mixture has turned golden brown. Serve immediately.

PASTITSO

Although Pastitso is really a Greek dish, because of its ingredients, it fits perfectly into the "Viva Italia" category.

2 pounds ground chuck
¾ pound butter
¼ cup diced onion
1 cup warm water
4 tablespoons tomato paste
1 12-ounce package macaroni
6 quarts rapidly boiling, slightly salted water
½ pound grated cheese; feta if you can get it, but mild American may be substituted
4 cups scalded milk
2 tablespoons cornstarch
2 tablespoons water
9 eggs, beaten until they are lemon colored
1 teaspoon salt
¼ teaspoon pepper
¼ teaspoon cinnamon

Brown the ground meat in two tablespoons of the butter. Add the onion and continue to cook until slightly glazed. Add the cup of water and tomato paste; cook for 5 minutes longer. Set aside to cool.

Boil the macaroni in the slightly salted water. Cook until it is nearly done. It should be a little on the tough side. Drain, and add ¼ pound of butter to the hot macaroni; stir in 5 tablespoonfuls of the cheese. Set aside until you make the sauce.

Melt the remaining butter in the hot milk. Mix the cornstarch with the two tablespoons of water and work into a paste. Stir this into the hot milk and butter and cook over a very low heat until thickened. Set aside to cool. Stir the eggs into the cooled cream sauce. Add the rest of the grated cheese, the salt, pepper and cinnamon.

Mix the hamburger and the macaroni together. Put half of this mixture into a 2-quart casserole. Pour half of the cream sauce and cheese over it. Add the rest of the macaroni and meat. Pour the remainder of the cream sauce over the top. Bake in a 350° F. oven for 1 hour. Serve piping hot.

SPAGHETTI WITH MEAT BALLS

Meat Balls

1 pound ground chuck (double ground, if your butcher will do it)
1 cup white-bread crumbs (do not use crusts), soaked in ½ cup water
1 tablespoon minced onion
1 clove garlic, minced
1 tablespoon chopped fresh parsley or 1 tablespoon dehydrated parsley
2 teaspoons salt
2 eggs
4 tablespoons olive oil

Sauce

2 medium-sized onions, peeled and sliced very thin
1 #2 can small Italian tomatoes
1 6-ounce can tomato paste
¾ cup warm water
2 tablespoons light brown sugar
¼ teaspoon basil
Pinch of thyme
Pinch of rosemary
Pinch of oregano
½ teaspoon salt
¼ teaspoon pepper

Spaghetti

1 pound spaghetti or spaghettini
6 quarts rapidly boiling slightly salted water
½ cup Parmesan cheese

Place the ground meat in a good-sized mixing bowl. Add the soaked bread crumbs (do not squeeze or drain). Add the onion, garlic, parsley and salt. Beat the eggs until they are lemon colored, and stir into the meat mixture. After dipping your hands in flour, form meat into balls about the size of golf balls. You should have about 12 of them.

Heat the olive oil in a skillet and brown the meat balls. (If you shake the pan from time to time they will stay nice and round.) After they are all browned, remove from the oil with a slotted spoon and set aside in a warm place.

To the olive oil which remains in the pan, add the slices of onion and cook until they are transparent. Then add the tomatoes, tomato paste, warm water and brown sugar. Stir and bring up to a simmer. Now add the basil, thyme, rosemary, oregano, salt and pepper and cover tightly. Let simmer for 45 minutes. At the end of this time, add the meat balls and cook for another 20 minutes.

Cook the spaghetti in the 6 quarts of water. Be sure it does not overcook. When done to the bite test, drain and place on a heated platter. Pour the meat balls and sauce over the mound of spaghetti. Serve the Parmesan cheese on the side as an additional garnish.

SPAGHETTI

4 strips very lean bacon, cut in ¼" pieces
1 pound ground chuck
3 onions, cut into ¼" slices
2 stalks celery, cut into ¼" pieces
2 carrots, diced
1 6-ounce can tomato paste
1 can chicken gumbo soup
½ cup white wine (optional)
2 cloves garlic, sliced very thin
½ teaspoon salt
4 twists of pepper mill
1 pinch of thyme
1 cup water or meat stock
1 pound spaghetti
6 quarts of rapidly boiling, slightly salted water
½ cup grated Parmesan-Romano cheese

Place the diced bacon in a deep skillet and brown. Add the ground chuck and continue to cook until it loses its reddish color. Add the onions, celery and carrots and continue to sauté until the onions and celery are glazed and transparent.

Add the tomato paste and soup. Then add the wine, garlic, salt, pepper, thyme and water or meat stock. Stir all very well, and let simmer for 45 minutes.

Cook the spaghetti in the 6 quarts of water. After 5 minutes of cooking, test spaghetti by biting one of the strands. Do not overcook. Drain the spaghetti, place on a heated platter, and pour the meat sauce over it. Sprinkle the cheese over the top. Serve immediately.

SPAGHETTI #2

This dish can be prepared far ahead of time and popped into the oven when needed. It freezes well, too, so it is a good one to have on hand when you're pressed for time.

1 tablespoon olive oil
1 pound ground chuck
1 small onion, chopped very fine
2 tablespoons catsup
1 8-ounce can mushroom stems and pieces (do not drain)
12 pitted black olives, sliced
1 can cream of mushroom soup
1 cup water
1 pound spaghetti
6 quarts rapidly boiling slightly salted water
½ cup buttered bread crumbs
3 tablespoons grated Parmesan cheese

Place the olive oil in a large skillet and sauté the ground chuck until it loses its red color. Add the onion, catsup, mushrooms with their liquid, black olives, soup and 1 cup of water. Bring to a simmer and continue to simmer while you are cooking the spaghetti.

Put the spaghetti in the 6 quarts of water. Cook for 5 minutes, then test by biting one of the strands. When the spaghetti has become slightly glazed and just a little tough to the taste, drain it and place it in a large mixing bowl. Pour the meat sauce over the spaghetti and mix together. Place all in a greased casserole dish. Mix the bread crumbs with the grated cheese and spread over the top.

Bake in a 350° F. oven for 40 minutes. The spaghetti finishes cooking during this time; if there is too much liquid left, return to the oven for a little while longer.

SPAGHETTI #3

Meat Balls

1 pound ground chuck
1 pound Italian sausage
2 cloves garlic, minced
½ cup bread crumbs
3 eggs, beaten to a lemon yellow
¼ cup flour
4 tablespoons olive oil

Sauce

2 cans tomato soup
3 tablespoons dehydrated onion flakes
1 cup water
1 teaspoon white sugar
Pinch of basil
½ teaspoon salt
¼ teaspoon pepper

Spaghetti

1 pound spaghetti
6 quarts rapidly boiling slightly salted water

Place the ground chuck in a large mixing bowl. Remove the sausages from their casings and add to the chuck. Add the garlic. Mix the bread crumbs with the eggs and let stand for a few minutes, until they are very soft. Add the bread crumbs and eggs to the meat mixture and mix thoroughly.

Form the meat mixture into small balls, using approximately a teaspoonful of meat for each. Roll them in the flour until they are coated. Heat the olive oil in a skillet and put in the meat balls. Shake the pan back and forth so they brown evenly on all sides. Add the tomato soup, onion flakes, water, sugar and basil. Add the salt and pepper and simmer for 30 minutes.

Cook the spaghetti in the 6 quarts of water. Do not overcook. Test by biting one of the strands after the first 5 minutes of cooking. When the spaghetti is done to your taste, put it on a heated platter and pour the meat balls and sauce over it. Serve immediately.

SPAGHETTI #4

¼ pound salt pork, cut into ¼″ cubes
½ pound ground chuck
1 clove garlic
1 medium onion, chopped fine
1 tablespoon dehydrated parsley
1 stalk celery, chopped fine
1 #2 can tomatoes
½ teaspoon salt
¼ teaspoon pepper
2 packages frozen green peas
1 pound vermacelli spaghetti
6 quarts rapidly boiling slightly salted water

Place the diced salt pork in a skillet and sauté until it is golden brown. Add the ground meat and continue to cook for 5 minutes. Add the garlic, onion, parsley and celery. Cook until the onion is glazed. Add the tomatoes, salt and pepper. Bring to a simmer and cook for 30 minutes.

Cook the spaghetti in the water. Test by biting a strand to see if it is done to your taste. When it is, remove from heat and add the frozen peas. Let the peas remain in the hot spaghetti and water for 5 minutes, then strain through a collander. Place the spaghetti and peas in a deep serving dish and pour the hot meat mixture over it. Mix lightly and serve.

SPAGHETTI #5

½ pound ground chuck
1 tablespoon olive oil
4 cups water
½ teaspoon salt
½ cup onion, diced into ¼″ pieces
1 8-ounce package thin spaghetti elbows
¼ teaspoon pepper
1 10½-ounce can condensed tomato soup

Brown the ground meat in the olive oil and set aside. Meanwhile, bring the water to a rolling boil, add the salt and onion. Add the spaghetti and continue to cook until it is almost done. Do not drain.

Add the browned meat to the spaghetti. Add the pepper. Continue to cook until the spaghetti is tender. Stir in the tomato soup. Simmer for 5 more minutes and then serve.

SPAGHETTI #6

½ pound ground chuck
½ pound ground veal
½ pound ground lean pork
½ cup pignolia nuts, chopped (you can get them from an
   Italian specialty store)
½ cup seedless raisins, chopped very fine
3 eggs, beaten to a lemon yellow
2 tablespoons olive oil
1 onion, diced in ½" pieces
1 clove garlic, cut very fine
1 #2 can Italian tomatoes
1 can tomato paste
¼ cup sugar
1 teaspoon salt
¼ teaspoon pepper
1 pound vermicelli spaghetti
12 quarts rapidly boiling slightly salted water

Mix the chuck, veal, pork, pignolia nuts, raisins and beaten eggs very thoroughly. Form into 1" diameter meat balls. Heat the olive oil in a large skillet; add the onion and garlic. Sauté for 5 minutes. Now brown the meat balls in the olive oil. Shake the pan from side to side to retain their shape and to assure even browning. When all the meat balls are browned, remove to a platter. Set aside.

Remove the onion and garlic from the olive oil with a slotted spoon and discard. Add the Italian tomatoes to the olive oil. Stir in the tomato paste, sugar, salt and pepper. Simmer over low heat for 1 hour. If the sauce gets too thick, add a little water. Twenty minutes before serving time, return the meat balls to the sauce and continue to simmer.

Cook the spaghetti in the water. Do not overcook; the spaghetti should be just tender enough to cut with a fork. Drain and place on a heated platter. Make an indentation in the center of the spaghetti and pour in the meat balls and sauce.

SPICED MEAT BALLS

½ pound ground chuck*
½ pound ground veal
½ pound ground pork
3 slices bread soaked in ½ cup milk
1 egg, slightly beaten
½ teaspoon salt
¼ teaspoon pepper
½ teaspoon allspice
¼ teaspoon nutmeg
2 tablespoons olive oil
1 24-ounce can V-8 vegetable juice
2 tablespoons cornstarch
¼ cup water
6 quarts rapidly boiling slightly salted water
1 pound spaghetti
¼ cup grated Parmesan-Romano cheese

Mix the beef, veal and pork thoroughly. When the bread has absorbed all of the milk, add the egg to it and mix into a thick paste. Add this to the meat and again mix well. Add the salt, pepper, allspice and nutmeg. Mix again. Form into meat balls about the size of golf balls.

Heat the olive oil in a skillet and brown the meat balls evenly on all sides. Add the V-8 juice and bring to a simmer. Let simmer for 30 minutes. Mix the cornstarch with the ¼ cup water and stir into the meat ball mixture to make it thicken. Be careful not to let it stick to the bottom of the pan.

Boil the spaghetti in the 6 quarts of water. Do not overcook; test the spaghetti by biting one of the strands after the first 5 minutes of cooking. When it is done to your taste, drain it and place it on a heated platter. Pour the meat balls and sauce over all. Sprinkle the cheese over the top, and serve.

* You can sometimes find chuck, veal and pork already mixed and sold in a package at the supermarket. If your local store sells it, you can buy it this way and save the trouble of mixing it yourself.

INDEX

A

Acorn squash, recipes featuring:
Hamburger-Filled Acorn
Squash, 47
Airtight containers, for freezing
hamburger, ix
Aluminum foil, for freezing
hamburger, x
Artichokes, recipes featuring:
Hamburger and Rice with
Artichokes, 144

B

Bacon Burger Surprise, 75
Basic Broth from Hamburger, 95
Basic Hamburger, A Good, 58
Basic hamburger, garnishes for,
60-61
Basic hamburger, variations for,
see Variations for basic
hamburger
Beans, recipes featuring:
Butter Bean-Hamburger Cas-
serole, 34
Chuck Wagon Western Bean
Casserole, 28
Hamburger Bean Soup, 100
Hamburger-Red Bean Soup,
98
Kidney Bean Special, 46
Lima Bean, Rice and Ham-
burger Loaf, 21
Meat Balls with Corn and
Beans, 125
Meat Loaf Ring with Creamed
Beans, 22

Belgian Hamburger Soup, 106
Bleu Cheese Burgers, 64
British Toads, 72
Broccoli, recipes featuring:
Meat Balls, Macaroni and
Broccoli, 52
Burger Sausage Rolls, 73
Burgers in Foil, 63
Butter Bean-Hamburger Casse-
role, 34

C

Cabbage Leaves Stuffed with
Hamburger, 53
Cabbage, recipes featuring:
Cabbage Leaves Stuffed with
Hamburger, 53
Hamburger-Cabbage Casse-
role, 36
Cauliflower Meat Loaf, 24
Cauliflower, recipes featuring:
Cauliflower Meat Loaf, 24
Hamburger Cauliflower Soup,
98
Richer Hamburger Cauli-
flower Soup, 99
Cheese, recipes featuring:
Bleu Cheese Burgers, 64
Hamburger Pizza, 86
Hamburger Stuffed Loaf, 81
Meat Loaf with Cheese, 11
Quick-and-Easy Sandwiches,
70
Chick Pea-Hamburger Loaf, 26
Chick Peas and Meat Balls, 119
Chick peas, recipes featuring:
Chick Pea-Hamburger Loaf,
26

Chick Peas and Meat Balls, 119

Chili, 107

Chili con Carne, 107

Chinese Chow Mein Loaf, 19

Chuck Wagon Western Bean Casserole, 28

Color, of good hamburger, ix

Corn, recipes featuring:
Meat Balls with Corn and Beans, 125

Curly Kale and Hamburger, 55

D

Danish Meat Pie, 94

Deer Hunter's Pie, 35

De Luxe Hamburger Pie, 85

Dutch Klopse, 123

Dutch Sauseasons, 74

E

Eat-More Casserole, 30

Egg-Burger Surprises, 89

Egg-Lemon Sauce, 129

Eggplant, Lamb and Cracked Wheat Casserole, 39

Eggplant, recipes featuring:
Eggplant, Lamb and Cracked Wheat Casserole, 39
Lamb-Eggplant Casserole, 128
Lamburgers with Eggplant, 132
Patlijan a la Naz, 137

F

Festive Meat Loaf, 17

Festive Meat Loaf #2, 23

Flank Steak Stuffed with Hamburger, 84

Freezing, of hamburger meat, ix

French Meat Loaf with Leek, 16

Freshness, of hamburger, ix

Fruit, recipes featuring:
Festive Meat Loaf, 17
Hamburger-Ham and Oranges, 55
Hamburger Mincemeat, 80
Lamburgers with Fresh Cran-

berries, 136

Lamb with Pomegranates, 132

Meat Loaf with Apple Sauce, 21

G

Garnishes for Basic Hamburger, 60-61

Glazed Burgers, 63

Good Basic Hamburger, A, 58

Greek Lamb Soup, 103

Green Rice with Hamburger, 110

Ground Lamb Turkey Stuffing, 92

Gypsy Lamb Stew, 130

H

Hamburger and Rice Casserole, 40

Hamburger and Rice with Artichokes, 144

Hamburger and Zucchini, 50

Hamburger Bake, 50

Hamburger Bean Soup, 100

Hamburger Breakfast Surprise, 108

Hamburger-Cabbage Casserole, 36

Hamburger Cauliflower Soup, 98

Hamburger Chowder, 97

Hamburger Chow Mein, 43

Hamburger Dumplings, 91

Hamburger Enchiladas, 48

Hamburger-Filled Acorn Squash, 47

Hamburger French Onion Soup, 96

Hamburger-French Pea Soup, 102

Hamburger-Ham and Oranges, 55

Hamburger, Herbs and Rice, 52

Hamburger Hot Pot, 27

Hamburger-Macaroni Pie, 76

Hamburger Meat Pudding, 89

Hamburger Mincemeat, 80

Hamburger Minestrone, 96

Hamburger Nests, 112
Hamburger Onion Pie, 90
Hamburger Oyster Casserole, 35
Hamburger Pancake Loaf, 25
Hamburger Pasties, 71
Hamburger Patties in Horse-
    Radish and Sour Cream
    Sauce, 54
Hamburger-Pea Soup, 106
Hamburger Pie Crust, 78
Hamburger Pizza, 86
Hamburger, Potato and Leek
    Soup, 104
Hamburger-Potato Soup, 100
Hamburger-Red Bean Soup, 98
Hamburger Scallopine, 140
Hamburger Shish Kabobs, 124
Hamburgers Made with Wine,
    69
Hamburger-Spinach Soup, 101
Hamburger Stuffed Loaf, 81
Hamburger-Stuffed Mushrooms,
    93
Hamburger Stuffing for Turkey
    or Chicken, 92
Hamburger with Corn Meal Bis-
    cuits, 51
Ham-Hamburger Meat Loaf, 14
Hearty Casserole, 37
Herb Burgers, 59
Hungarian Burgers, 59
Hungarian Meat Ball Soup, 104

I

Indian Burgers, 59
Italian Burgers, 59
Italian Rice, 139

K

Kale, recipes featuring:
    Curly Kale and Hamburger,
    55
Kidney Bean Special, 46

L

Lamb and Rice, 130
Lamb Cakes, 133
Lamb-Eggplant Casserole, 128

Lamb in Grape Leaves, 129
Lamb, nutritional value of, 62
Lamb Pilaf, 127
Lamb Shish Kabobs, 135
Lamb Soup, 126
Lamb-Spinach Soup, 105
Lamb Stew, Turkish Style, 131
Lamburgers, 62
Lamburgers, Indian Style, 136
Lamburgers with Eggplant, 132
Lamburgers with Fresh Cran-
    berries, 136
Lamburgers with Lemon Sauce,
    134
Lasagne #1, 142
Lasagne #2, 143
Leek, recipes featuring:
    French Meat Loaf with Leek,
    16
    Hamburger, Potato and Leek
    Soup, 104
Lima Bean, Rice and Hambur-
    ger Loaf, 21
Little Meat Loaves, 56

M

Macaroni and Meat Balls, 140
Madrid Rice Casserole, 29
Meat Ball-Beer Casserole, 32
Meat Balls in Caraway, 117
Meat Balls in Mustard Sauce,
    118
Meat Balls in Red Wine, 115
Meat Balls, Macaroni and Broc-
    coli, 52
Meat Balls with Corn and Beans,
    125
Meat Balls with Pine Nuts, 123
Meat Balls with Sauerbraten
    Gravy, 116
Meat Balls with Sweet and Sour
    Mushrooms, 122
Meat Loaf with Apple Sauce, 21
Meat Loaf with Cheese, 11
Meat Loaf with Creamed Beans,
    22
Meat Loaf with Mushroom
    Soup, 18
Meat Loaf with Yoghurt, 23
Mexican Casserole, 36

Mexican Hamburger and Rice, 49
Milk-Rich Meat Loaf, 12
Mushrooms, recipes featuring:
Hamburger-Stuffed Mushrooms, 93
Meat Balls with Sweet and Sour Mushrooms, 122

N

Nogales Tamale Pie, 87
Nuts, recipes featuring:
Meat Balls with Pine Nuts, 123
Walnut-Meat Ball Casserole, 30

O

Okra, recipes featuring:
Okra with Lamb, 131
Okra with Lamb, 131
Olives, recipes featuring:
Ripe Olive Hamburger Casserole, 33
One-Dish Meal, 45
Onion Hamburger Stew, 41
Onions and Hamburger, Milan Style, 44
Onions, recipes featuring:
Hamburger French Onion Soup, 96
Hamburger Onion Pie, 90
Onion Hamburger Stew, 41
Onions and Hamburger, Milan Style, 44
Onions Stuffed with Hamburger, 56

P

Pasta, generic name for macaroni, 138
Pasta, how to cook, 138
Pasta, recipes featuring:
Hamburger-Macaroni Pie, 76
Lasagne #1, 142
Lasagne #2, 143
Macaroni and Meat Balls, 140
Meat Balls, Macaroni and Broccoli, 52

Spaghetti, 147
Spaghetti #2, 148
Spaghetti #3, 149
Spaghetti #4, 150
Spaghetti #5, 150
Spaghetti #6, 151
Spaghetti with Meat Balls, 146
Spiced Meat Balls, 152
Pastitso, 145
Patlijan a la Naz, 137
Peas, recipes featuring:
Hamburger-French Pea Soup, 102
Hamburger-Pea Soup, 106
Pecan Burgers, 59
Pelmeny, or Meat Dumplings, 77
Pimentos with Paprika Hamburger, 91
Pizza with Hamburger, 141
Potatoes, recipes featuring:
Hamburger, Potato and Leek Soup, 104
Hamburger-Potato Soup, 100
Raw Potato Casserole, 37
Steak and Potatoes, 57

Q

Quick-and-Easy Pizza Sandwiches, 70
Quick Hamburger Goulash, 49
Quickie Cutlets, 108
Quick Meat Pie, 109
Quick Meat Sauce over Rice, 111

R

Raw Potato Casserole, 37
Red Letter Day Casserole, 31
Rice, Hamburger and Zucchini, 139
Rice, recipes featuring:
Green Rice with Hamburger, 110
Hamburger and Rice Casserole, 40
Hamburger and Rice with Artichokes, 144

Hamburger, Herbs and Rice, 52
Italian Rice, 139
Lamb and Rice, 130
Madrid Rice Casserole, 29
Quick Meat Sauce over Rice, 111
Rice, Hamburger and Zucchini, 139
Sage and Rice Hamburger, 110
Sweet and Sour Meat Balls with Rice, 114
Wild Rice and Hamburger Casserole, 38
Richer Hamburger Cauliflower Soup, 99
Ripe Olive Hamburger Casserole, 33
Russian Meat Loaf, 15

S

Sage and Rice Hamburger, 110
Sauces, recipes featuring:
Glazed Burgers, 63
Hamburger Patties in Horse-Radish and Sour Cream Sauce, 54
Lamburgers with Lemon Sauce, 134
Meat Balls in Mustard Sauce, 118
Meat Balls with Sauerbraten Gravy, 116
Schnitzel Burgers, 67
Self-Glazing Meat Loaf, 20
Serbian Meat Balls, 118
Sesame Burgers, 62
Simple Meat Loaf, 18
Sloppier Joes, 66
Sloppiest Joes, 67
Sloppy Joe, 66
Spaghetti, 147
Spaghetti #2, 148
Spaghetti #3, 149
Spaghetti #4, 150
Spaghetti #5, 150
Spaghetti #6, 151
Spaghetti with Meat Balls, 147

Spanish Hamburgers, 68
Spanish Sloppy Joes, 68
Spiced Meat Balls, 152
Spices, recipes featuring:
Lamburgers, Indian Style, 136
Meat Balls in Caraway, 117
Pimentos with Paprika Hamburger, 91
Sage and Rice Hamburgers, 110
Sesame Burgers, 62
Spiced Meat Balls, 152
Spices, substitution of, x
Spinach, recipes featuring:
Hamburger-Spinach Soup, 101
Lamb-Spinach Soup, 105
Spinach Soup with Hamburger, 102
Spinach Soup with Hamburger, 102
Sorbonne Sandwiches, 70
Steak and Potatoes, 57
Stretch-that-Meat Burgers, 59
Stuffed Tomatoes, Italian Style, 42
Stuffing, hamburger used for:
Flank Steak Stuffed with Hamburger, 84
Ground Lamb Turkey Stuffing, 92
Hamburger Stuffing for Turkey or Chicken, 92
Veal Breast Stuffed with Hamburger, 84
Swedish Meat Balls, 120
Swedish Meat Balls #2, 120
Swedish Meat Balls #3, 121
Swedish Meat Balls in Crusts, 82
Sweet and Sour Meat Balls with Rice, 114

T

Teen-Agers' Special Sandwiches, 65
Teens' Rib Liners, 65
Tiny Hamburgers, 79
Tomatoes, recipes featuring:
Stuffed Tomatoes, Italian Style, 42

Tomatoes with Filling, 109
Tucson Meat Pie, 23

W

Walnut Burgers, 59
Walnut-Meat Ball Casserole, 30
Western-Style Meat Balls, 124
Wheaties Meat Loaf with Vege-
    table Soup, 13
Wild Rice and Hamburger Cas-
    serole, 38
Wine, recipes featuring:
    Hamburgers Made with Wine,
    69
    Meat Balls in Red Wine, 115

U

Upside-Down Sandwiches, 64

Y

Yamburgers, 34
Yoghurt, recipes featuring:
    Meat Loaf with Yoghurt, 23

V

Variations for basic hamburger:
    Cashew Burgers, 59
    Cheesits, 59
    Herb Burgers, 59
    Hungarian Burgers, 59
    Indian Burgers, 59
    Italian Burgers, 59
    Pecan Burgers, 59
    Stretch-that-Meat Burgers, 59
    Walnut Burgers, 59
    Zippy Burgers, 59
Veal Breast Stuffed with Ham-
    burger, 88
Veal Loaf, 19

Z

Zippy Burgers, 59
Zucchini, recipes featuring:
    Hamburger and Zucchini, 50
    Rice, Hamburger and Zuc-
    chini, 139

$1,000 AWARD

FOR YOUR FAVORITE RECIPE

A recipe you are using right now or one that may have been in the family for generations may be just what we're looking for. We're reviewing recipes for the next edition of Potpourri of Cookery. Recipes submitted and approved may be published in this unique cookbook made up entirely of these great recipes.

We would like to review your recipe and if approved you are eligible to win one of our CASH AWARDS UP TO $1,000. Please send only one recipe entry per family (any kind are eligible from appetizers to desserts).

We're not looking for recipes from professional chefs. A simple recipe may be the next winner—let us be the judge. The review service is free, easy way to find out if your recipe is a winner.

FREE ENTRY COUPON
ON OTHER SIDE

MAIL TO

TREASURED RECIPE CONTEST
ATTN: FLEET & MORGAN
       200 MADISON AVENUE
       NEW YORK, NY 10016
YES!   Please enter my recipe and notify me if it
       is accepted for Publication.

Name _____
               (please print clearly)

Address _____

City _____

State _____ Zip _____

_____
             NAME OF MY RECIPE